Can Gorbachev Change the Soviet Union?

Published in cooperation with
the Austrian Institute
for International Affairs

Can Gorbachev Change the Soviet Union?

The International Dimensions of Political Reform

Zdenek Mlynar

Translated by Marian Sling
and Ruth Tosek

Westview Press
BOULDER / SAN FRANCISCO / OXFORD

DK 288
M 59
1990

Copyright © 1990 by Westview Press, Inc.

Published in 1990 in the United States of America by Westview Press, Inc., 5500 Central Avenue, Boulder, Colorado 80301, and in the United Kingdom by Westview Press, Inc., 36 Lonsdale Road, Summertown, Oxford OX2 7EW

Library of Congress Cataloging in Publication Data
Mlynář, Zdeněk.
    Can Gorbachev change the Soviet Union? : the international dimensions of political reform / Zdeněk Mlynář ; translated by Marian Sling and Ruth Tosek.
    p. cm.
    Translated from the German.
    ISBN 0-8133-0934-4
    1. Soviet Union—Politics and government—1985- .
2. Soviet Union—Foreign relations—1985- . I. Title.
DK288.M59   1990
327.47—dc20   89-70637
                                                                  CIP

Printed and bound in the United States of America

       The paper used in this publication meets the requirements
⊗   of the American National Standard for Permanence of Paper
       for Printed Library Materials Z39.48-1984.

10   9   8   7   6   5   4   3   2   1

Contents

Preface

This book was conceived and written at the time of the Nineteenth All-Union Conference of the Communist Party of the Soviet Union in the summer of 1988. The manuscript was finalized in the spring of 1989. The English edition comes out a full year later—a year that was marked by stormy developments in the Soviet Union and in the entire Soviet bloc and brought some far-reaching and important systemic changes. It is therefore impossible to update the text through additions and corrections.

The original main purpose of the study was to analyze the specifically Soviet historical and ideological conditions for a change of the system that could take place without dangerous disruptions. I intended to describe an optimal and realistic program for systemic change and at the same time to point out the limitations of any change that is mainly imposed from above.

At the time it was still correct to argue that Gorbachev's principal problem consisted in mobilizing sufficient popular pressure against the bureaucratic system. But during the year 1989 this pressure "from below" manifested itself in extreme forms of mass unrest, such as strikes, mass demonstrations, and in some cases nationalistic conflicts marked by violence and pogroms. In the smaller East European countries we witnessed an extraordinarily rapid disintegration of the Soviet-type system. It is therefore no longer possible today to speak about the existence of a "bloc" as I do it in Chapter 3 in the section on the impact of reform on the Soviet bloc.

Some tendencies and conflicts that had already been noticeable earlier and that are described in this study have, at the beginning of 1990, not only acquired great momentum but also become so interrelated that they form a veritable Gordian knot. The fate of Gorbachev's reform politics will depend on whether it will be possible to unravel this knot, gradually, without disruptions, and through compromise. In the area of politics, the nationalist problem has become much more serious and important than I have described it. In my study I did not make it a separate object of analysis but dealt with it only in the context of the representation of interests.

In spite of all these limitations, I believe that the study might help the reader to understand the developments in the Soviet Union. Some parts of the study might be overtaken by events, but the book as a whole represents a valid in-depth analysis of the Soviet system and a description of possible scenarios for future developments that are only applicable to the Soviet Union and cannot be measured by Western standards. This applies to the history predating Gorbachev's reform efforts as well as to the specific developments of institutional structures, such as the rule of law in the Soviet system. I also believe that the analysis of the role of the Communist party remains valid, in spite of tendencies toward the formation of other parties.

If it should turn out that the pace of change will increase further, bringing more democracy earlier to the Soviet Union than I anticipated in my cautious analysis, I will still be happier than in the opposite case.

Zdenek Mlynar

Introduction

In 1985 Gorbachev assumed the highest political post in the Soviet Union. Since then, a host of books has been written on the subject, together with a vast number of articles, studies, and commentaries on what his new policy means and what it does not mean, on what it can or cannot change in the USSR as well as in the rest of the world. There is no need today to put forward specific arguments supporting the contention that Gorbachev's policy is a genuine endeavor for change. Only an insignificant minority of analysts would claim that this policy is nothing but a tactical maneuver to conceal an unchanging reality. Gorbachev is serious about his policy of *perestroika* (restructuring)—on this there is increasing agreement even in the West. Yet the question as to what its content will be remains open.

There can be no doubt that Gorbachev and his group within the leadership of the Communist Party of the Soviet Union (CPSU) really intend to change existing conditions both in domestic policy and in the sphere of international relations. But there is no straightforward reply to questions regarding the direction and extent of this change—nor to the question of whether Gorbachev will be able to achieve all he hopes to achieve. He is limited by an entire spectrum of conditions, only some of which are obvious; others remain more or less concealed, and their significance is not always quite clear.

In this study I want to focus attention precisely on this spectrum of conditions. My intention is to outline the possibilities for qualitative changes in the Soviet system and the limits to reforms, at least for the foreseeable future.

I also want to focus attention on problems that cannot be judged according to ideas current in the West, because in the USSR the same concepts may have, and in fact often do have, a different meaning. I believe that it is important, when discussing these ideas, to point to at least the main historical factors that can determine the prospects for radical reforms in the existing economic, social, and political system. In my opinion, these are not confined to factors originating mainly in the years of Stalin's totalitarian dictatorship; a number are also linked with the history of Russia, whose cultural and political traditions differ from those that have shaped developments in the West.

Unless these and similar matters are taken into account, it is not possible to answer the question of whether Gorbachev has even a chance of changing the Soviet system successfully or whether he will meet the same fate as Khrushchev or the reform communists of Poland, Hungary, or Czechoslovakia. Moreover, it is in these fundamental aspects of Soviet reality that we can see how far Soviet society and its political leadership has proven successful or not in coming to terms with the past—with the assessment of their own history. Only in this context is it possible to attempt an analysis of the relationships among the economy, politics, and ideology in the course of the reforms now under way.

Up to now, Western analysts have paid little attention to a separate issue—namely, the need and possibility for changes in the institutional political system of the USSR. In the crudest terms, this issue is generally discussed in the West as the problem of the one-party monopoly; and an answer is usually sought by speculating as to whether it is possible to anticipate the emergence of a system of more than one political party—a party in power and an opposition according to the pattern of West European parliamentary traditions.

I believe that to put the question this way is to vastly oversimplify the matter. More to the point, the question is whether and under what conditions the different interests, needs, and aspirations of the various social groups that make up the "reality" of Soviet society can be formulated and expressed within the institutional structure of the political system in the USSR.

In my view this problem cannot be solved simply by referring to the existence of different political parties. But it is a problem whose solution is of fundamental importance for the future of the Soviet system: If the qualitative changes programmed by Gorbachev are to become truly irreversible, and if they are to be independent of the personalities of the party and state leadership, they must be anchored institutionally. If such anchoring does not occur, the changes in the political system will necessarily remain provisional.

The third set of questions to be discussed in this study relates to Soviet foreign policy, or, more precisely, the Soviet concept of relations between the Soviet system and the "rest of the world," with the possibility of cooperation (or conflict) between the Soviet system and other economic and political systems in today's world. Can the nature of this complex of relations, known in simplified terms as East-West relations, be changed? Can relations between East and West essentially be demilitarized? Can demilitarization be achieved by the USSR, a world superpower precisely (or even exclusively) *because* of its military power and not because of its economic efficiency or political attractiveness? Can the present character of relations within the Soviet bloc, which have more than once proved to be based largely on Soviet military strength (as in 1956 and 1968), be changed without endangering the superpower position of the USSR?

The answers to these and similar questions surely do not depend solely on the intentions of Gorbachev and his political leadership. Nor do they depend unilaterally on political steps taken by the Soviet side. And yet the Soviets' behavior is a decisive factor for possible change in this international context, because it is the Soviet side that is declaring its intention to change existing practices and advance along a new path. It is for this reason that we shall discuss these issues—and the opportunities offered by new developments—from the Soviet perspective.

These issues are treated here in terms of politics and possible political changes. Questions concerning economic matters are dealt with only in this political context. Although transformations in the economic sphere are certainly important to the fate of the reforms as a whole, it is beyond the author's power to make an analysis of the questions pertaining to the Soviet economy, the mechanism of economic management, the relationship between the plan and the market, and the problems that are linked with the Soviet's attempts to find solutions to its present economic crisis. The reader must seek answers to these and similar questions in the very extensive literature now available.[1]

The object of this study is not to foretell the future. Nor is it possible to provide unequivocal answers to all of the questions posed in this volume. At times, merely the formulation of a question may well be useful; at other times, it may be important to highlight more than one possible answer to a given question, even when it is impossible to say with certainty which alternative will be realized.

In some cases I have tried to overcome the bad habit, widespread in the West, of applying our own standard of judgment on reforms that, by necessity, emanate from a totally different political system. Gorbachev's reforms, their objectives and possibilities, successes and failures, cannot be measured by a Western yardstick; they can be judged only within the context of the Soviet past and present. It is by this means only that we can consider the future without losing touch with existing reality.

Even as the reforms are carried out, development in the USSR will continue to follow a specific course in accordance with Soviet (Russian) conditions and possibilities. But the features most open to development will be those that correspond, on the whole, to the common interests and needs of various societies in the world today—those that ameliorate conflict situations and promote cooperative relations between the Soviet system and other systems.

In order to achieve the objective of cooperative relations, both sides must refrain from harboring illusions. Such realism, I believe, is compatible with an optimistic view of the future.

1 / What Can a Radical Reform Mean in the USSR?

The chapter title poses the question I address throughout this book, not only in the first chapter. But subsequent chapters deal with specific problems: which changes are realistically possible in an institutional political system, and which are possible in the sphere of international relations. This chapter deals more with a general view as to what is (or is not) possible in the USSR should Gorbachev's policy be totally successful.

Even in this case, of course, we cannot expect more than political changes can offer—to say nothing of changes carried out in a relatively short period of time. So, in posing the question of radical reform, I have in mind a period of roughly ten years—in other words, a foreseeable period (at least in terms of its characteristic features).

Gorbachev and Previous Attempts at Reform

The Soviet system must be reformed if developments are not to lead to insoluble contradictions and crises—so the Soviet leadership acknowledged some thirty years ago, after Stalin's death. And, in fact, several attempts at reforming the Soviet system have been made—both in the USSR itself under Nikita Khrushchev and in other Soviet-bloc countries (in Poland and Hungary in 1956, in Czechoslovakia in 1968, and in Poland in 1980–1981). Other countries outside the Soviet bloc—countries whose original political orientation basically coincided with the "Soviet model" of economic, social, and political development—have at various times tried to introduce substantial changes and deviations from this model. Such efforts were made, in particular, by Yugoslavia after 1948 and by China after 1958.

The past thirty years have yielded a wealth of experience with attempts at reform; it is therefore understandable that Gorbachev's current policies are often compared to this past experience. Such a comparison tends to arouse pessimism, however, because—with the exception of China, where reforms are only now being introduced and have not yet been completed—all other attempts have failed (albeit for a variety of reasons and in entirely different forms). It is easy to arrive at the conclusion that Gorbachev, like his predecessors, must also fail.

Although the history of the Soviet system undoubtedly offers more than enough cause for pessimistic forecasts, Gorbachev's present attempt at reform cannot be identified with earlier attempts. Set off against the many similarities is a whole series of differences—some of which strongly suggest that the bad experiences of the past need not necessarily be repeated.

A direct analogy to the smaller Soviet-bloc countries— Poland, Hungary, or Czechoslovakia—is out of the question. Attempts at reform in those countries failed mainly because they were prevented from setting out on their independent paths, and because the decisive blows to their reform efforts were delivered by outside forces. I am not referring merely to the outright Soviet military intervention in Hungary in 1956 or in Czechoslovakia in 1968 but more broadly to the decisive dependence of these countries on the USSR and to the overall situation in the entire Soviet bloc that, in the final analysis, put insurmountable obstacles in the way of these reforms. The two open military interventions highlighted this restriction. But even where such intervention did not take place, attempts at reform were essentially restricted by the situation in the USSR and throughout the bloc—not only in Poland in 1957–1958 and again in 1980–1981, but also in Hungary after 1968 and in the German Democratic Republic (GDR) throughout its history.

One of the major reasons for the conflict between the isolated attempts at reform in the smaller Soviet-bloc countries, on the one hand, and the interests of the USSR and the entire bloc, on the other, was the fact that in those smaller countries attempts at reforming the Soviet-type system were always (though to differing degrees) linked with endeavors to attain greater independence from Moscow. All European Soviet-bloc countries reached a point in their histories that marked the end of any chance that they would carry out, independently and with full sovereignty, their own particular policy of "building socialism." Roughly speaking, this point occurred somewhere in the first postwar years (1947–1948 at the earliest). It coincided with sweeping political changes that marked the beginning of the usually enforced process of Sovietization—that is, the imposition of a Soviet-type economic, social, and political system without regard for the stage of development, the historic traditions, or the will of the majority of the population in the country involved.

What has since been called the process of "building socialism" has, of course, taken place in each of the European Soviet-bloc countries under different conditions.[2] Certain differences are of an entirely fundamental nature, especially those pertaining to developments in the immediate postwar period. In some of these countries it would have been inconceivable for the Communist party to have gained the leading position of power (let alone a monopoly of power) without the decisive role of the Soviet army. This clearly applies to the countries defeated in the war, such as the GDR, Hungary, and Romania. But it also applies to Poland. However, in countries such as Czechoslovakia, Yugoslavia, and, perhaps to some extent, Bulgaria, the situation was entirely different; the communists enjoyed considerable influence, and the possibility of "building socialism" did not depend to any significant extent on the presence of the Soviet army (a presence that ended after 1945 in both Czechoslovakia and Yugoslavia).

Irrespective of these differences, it can be said that after Stalin's death, these countries' attempts at reforming the imposed Soviet system always entailed specific efforts to return to their own independent development prior to the forced Sovietization. In the USSR itself (and generally also in the neighboring countries of the bloc, where no reforms happened to be under way), these efforts have hitherto been described as attempts at "counter-revolution," a "return to capitalism," and so forth—and, hence, have always provided the justification for all measures aimed at suppressing any moves toward reform.

The label "return to capitalism" was also applied to steps taken to restore ways of life that had existed before the forcible Sovietization of a given country. Granted, some of these steps have been linked in the past with capitalist economic and social conditions. But this is not to say that their observance would inevitably lead to the restoration of these conditions; for after years of Soviet-type development, the economic or class foundations for a reintroduction of capitalism no longer existed.

Attempts at reform in the smaller Soviet-bloc countries have generally focused on two sets of problems: a greater role for the market in the economy (or the possibility of a multisector economy, but with state and cooperative ownership clearly dominant), and elements of political pluralism (linked both with the right of various social groups to organize politically and with the mechanism of parliamentary democracy). Each country, however, has dealt with these problems in its own way and within the context of its own tradition. Czechoslovakia, for example, fell back on practical experience with a functioning pluralist democracy in 1918–1938, whereas Hungary had more experience with an authoritarian regime. As the traditions of such countries clashed with the Soviet model, individual means had to be found to effect reforms utilizing these traditions—but without tinkering unduly with the Soviet model. Moscow perceived such efforts as "counter-revolution," however, because the concept of "revolution" was identified exclusively with Sovietization.

Problems of this type do not threaten Gorbachev's policy. His policy is an attempt at reform in the "mother country" of the Soviet system—a country accustomed not only to dealing with all its problems in its own way but also to dictating its will in these matters to other countries in the bloc, a country that sees itself as the model of "socialism" and "revolution" (or "socialist revolution"). The reforms in Czechoslovakia in 1968 were labeled "right wing opportunism." Identical reforms in the USSR today are viewed as "creative Leninism." Only the terminology has changed.

This advantage is, however, balanced by a disadvantage, in the sense that Gorbachev's reform policy cannot refer to a point in the past that would form an organic and logical link with present political developments. For the present generation of Soviet citizens, there exists no memory of any other system. But that system must be changed; if it is not, the results will be stagnation, crisis, or even collapse. Soviet society today has no idea how a market economy functions; nor can it imagine the workings of pluralist democracy (a system that, in fact, has never existed throughout the history of the major regions of the USSR). Yet not even Gorbachev's reform can do without certain elements of both the market and the pluralist interests.

To be sure, Gorbachev is in no danger of ending up like Dubcek. Whereas Dubcek's major problem was to keep within acceptable boundaries the pressure for democratization coming "from below," Gorbachev's main challenge is to muster—"from below"—sufficiently strong pressure against the bureaucratic system, and to win the support of the widest possible social strata for his radical reform.

Gorbachev's challenge is distinguished from the reform process in China by the fact that the Soviet system has ruled for so long in the USSR that its society cannot remember any alternative. In China a decisive change in the countryside—involving perhaps 80 percent of the population—was initiated in 1978 simply by removing the bans and directives imposed by the system of communes and the policy of "cultural revolution" (before that, it was the policy of central planning). Once this had been accomplished, the Chinese farmers knew how to work more efficiently, how to sell their produce on the local market, and so on. One of China's fundamental problems—ensuring basic supplies of food—was thus solved.

A similar situation confronted Lenin in Soviet Russia when, a few years after the revolution and the brief period of "war communism," he introduced the New Economic Policy (NEP), which enabled farmers to work again for themselves. But the situation in the USSR today is quite different: Gorbachev's endeavor to give the kolkhoz and its members the scope in which to show economic entrepreneurial initiative has encountered a decided lack of interest "from below." There is no one living today who would be capable of or accustomed to working without the directives of the command system that the reform aims to abolish.[3] Here we are talking merely about the most elementary problem, about the simplest form of "enterprise"—agriculture. Given that the same factor (i.e., the absence of experience and of any desire to work in ways other than those demanded by the existing system) prevails in Soviet industry and technology, it is easy to see how enormous is the obstacle facing any attempt at a radical transformation of the system.

This obstacle is the result of roughly sixty years of development. If Gorbachev hopes to overcome it, he too will have to look for a stage in the past that can serve as a point of departure, at least in people's minds. This is precisely the rationale behind his use of the slogan "Back to Lenin"—that is, back to the theory and practice of the 1920s, when Lenin was still alive. By the same token, however, the USSR will have to face up to a critical analysis of the entire history of the Soviet system. Of course, such an analysis is bound to recall Khrushchev's attempt at overcoming the Stalinist past; it also raises the question, Will Gorbachev end up like Khrushchev?

I believe he need not end up like Khrushchev. True, there is no guarantee that he will break down the barriers erected over the past sixty years. But a repetition of Khrushchev's fate is not inevitable. Apart from certain similarities, there are many fundamental differences between the reform policy of Gorbachev and that pursued by Khrushchev with respect to policy goals, content, and methods as well as the conditions under which it was introduced.

Following Stalin's death, the mechanism of mass political terror had become problematic. Police surveillance and repression as the major methods of governing could no longer deal satisfactorily with the pressing economic and social problems facing Soviet society at the time. Thus Khrushchev's task was relatively simple, at least at the outset: He had to eliminate mass political terror as a method of governing. The result, of course, was a conflict with the power mechanisms that carried out this terror; but these mechanisms represented only a section of the power apparatus against which the rest of the bureaucracy and the power elite found it easy to unite. By that time, Stalin's system of terror was already threatening the interests of everyone, including the power elite itself.

The reform under Khrushchev was confined to a handful of simple measures in the economic and social sphere.[4] The priority given to heavy industry (a tradition under Stalin) was abandoned, whereas the consumer goods industry, agriculture, and basic social services (including housing) were expanded. The consequence was (limited) decentralization of management in these spheres.

Khrushchev announced radical change, but he never carried it out. His propaganda set forth the gigantic task of catching up with and overtaking the most advanced capitalist states in both the economic and the social spheres—in production as well as in living standards. Since the Khrushchev era, the Soviet system had been justifying itself to the population by claiming that it was capable of expanding the manufacturing and consumer industries better than any other system. This criterion, of secondary importance under Stalin (i.e., subordinated to ideological formulas about the class struggle in the USSR and in the world), was for Khrushchev the triumph of communism. It meant the building of a modern industrial society based on scientific and technological progress of the same type as that in advanced capitalist countries, but with higher living standards for the working people and more effective satisfaction of their needs.

Even after Khrushchev's downfall, the Soviet power elite did not dare to renounce these aims openly. The aims remained on paper, however—and, in practice, genuine progress in the development of a modern industrial society became less and less important as a measure of Soviet power. During the Brezhnev era, it was the mechanism of economic management in particular that was gradually seen to be in jeopardy, as it became less and less capable of achieving the goals set by its own leadership. Indeed, the methods by which Soviet society has been governed thus far are incapable of solving the key problem of transition from extensive to intensive economic development.

The problems that Khrushchev dealt with by making ideological pronouncements are the same problems Gorbachev must tackle by radically transforming the economic management system of the USSR. Gorbachev's task is thus incomparably more difficult than Khrushchev's. If (like Khrushchev) Gorbachev were to be toppled by an alliance of anti-reform forces, the USSR would be seen as abandoning its fundamental objective—to build a modern industrial society capable of standing up to competition with the West. Yet not even the Brezhnev administration dared to retract this objective.

The development of a modern industrial society in the USSR is inevitable. The consciousness of the Soviet people has already progressed too far to be turned back.

Khrushchev was overthrown in 1964 by an alliance of forces in the power elite who, though not favoring a return to the methods of Stalin's dictatorship, were afraid of further experiments and reforms that might endanger their privileged social position. After his overthrow, Khrushchev was accused of having failed to implement his professed aims (a claim that was true to some extent), of being too subjective, of taking ill-considered actions, and of undermining the stability of the system while failing to attain promised objectives. But Soviet society—especially the economy—still possessed certain reserves that could be mobilized, after the elimination of mass political terror, to achieve some economic successes—even though the traditional policy of extensive economic development had barely changed. This trend continued into the mid-1970s.[5] Were it not for this stagnation camouflaged as progress, Khrushchev's overthrow could never have led to anything other than the rapid onset of crisis.

Today the Soviet economy no longer possesses such reserves. Gorbachev has made this clear on several occasions: There is no alternative to his reform program except stagnation and backwardness.[6] A further temporary stabilization of the whole Soviet system can be achieved not by postponing reforms but only by implementing them. After the experience of the last few years of Brezhnev's rule (followed by the brief period of Chernyenko's rule), most members of the Soviet elite are also fully aware of this situation. Gorbachev's overthrow could not lead to a "return to Brezhnevism," because such a return is no longer possible; it would inevitably lead to economic and political crisis. Thus it is hardly conceivable at present that an alliance strong enough to topple Gorbachev could emerge in the Soviet power structure. There may well be disagreements within the elite about the shape of the reform (which even the power elite now acknowledges as being inevitable), about what it should involve, and at what pace it should proceed. But the situation is nothing like that at the end of 1964, when most of the elite wanted an end to all reform experiments.

The fact that it is no longer possible to stabilize the system by suspending the reforms is evident even in the new distribution of social forces in the USSR. Whereas in Khrushchev's day the ratio of the urban and rural population was roughly 1:1, today it is 2:1 in favor of the cities. Moreover, the standard of education has risen sharply, resulting not only in higher qualifications but also in higher ambitions of people regarding the management of their work and their lives.[7] People with a full secondary education (i.e., graduates of technical schools or universities) cannot be governed by the same methods as those used on backward Russian villagers who arrived in the newly emerging cities in the 1930s and 1940s. During Khrushchev's rule, all Soviet citizens labored under the direct experience of Stalin's mass terror, and this memory governed their actions and aspirations. Nowadays, however, the majority of Soviet people were either children when Stalin died or were born later. Even today's elite consists for the most part of people who generally reached political maturity after Stalin's time. A considerable number of these individuals have received a higher education.

So, compared with earlier attempts to reform the system (specifically, those made in the Soviet-bloc countries after Stalin's death), Gorbachev's efforts have two advantages that justify his hopes for success: First, as the need for reform is an internal necessity, it cannot be destroyed from the outside; and, second, any break in the reform process would be seen by both the general population and the elite as an open invitation to stagnation and economic crisis that would spread throughout all spheres of society. Thus Gorbachev is in a unique position.

At the same time, however, the factors offering the hope that attempts at reform in the USSR will not again be blocked by the overthrow of the reform-oriented party leader probably also make for a very long-term contradictory advance, full of conflict and compromise. The success of Gorbachev's reforms can be envisioned only as a long-drawn-out process that will pass through various stages. The first and most foreseeable stage (in the best-case scenario) may be the final removal of the forces capable of directly threatening the reform and, after a period of time, of attempting to stop it. During this phase, doors will also be opened to further fundamental changes— changes attainable only in the long term (roughly ten or more years). Certain aspects of such qualitative changes— such as an economic dynamism capable of ensuring scientific and technological progress in the production process and comparable with the West, or a properly functioning system of political democracy and self-administration in the decisionmaking process—are tasks for more than one generation.

The Past and Its Role in the Reform Process of the USSR

As noted, the present economic, social, and political system of the USSR is the product of developments over a sixty-year span. This system, however, did not emerge from a void. It was rooted in economic, social, and political conditions and potentialities, whose sources, in turn, were not rooted simply in the 1917 revolution but had been formed over centuries during the historical development of the Russian empire.

Certain fundamental characteristics of the system that Gorbachev wants to change by means of his radical reform so that it will be in tune, not with the past but with the present and future, are deeply rooted in historical traditions from which the present system emerged. Of course, there are significant differences between the needs, interests, and goals of pre-revolutionary Russia and those of post-revolutionary Russia. Yet one cannot ignore certain crucial similarities, especially in the development of the political system. These common features can best be explained by noting that, before the revolution as well as after it, the dominant trend was authoritarian, dictatorial decisionmaking from the center as opposed to policymaking based on decentralization and self-administration. Moreover, both before and after the revolution, state power was seen as the decisive force in the organization of society. The state itself was seen primarily as an instrument capable of coercing various social forces to act "in the interest of the community." The structure of civil society was not only relatively underdeveloped but also was essentially subordinated to the state (i.e., the political regime). Civil society itself had only a small measure of autonomy vis-à-vis the government, and its different various components had only a small degree of autonomy and autonomous interaction within the society.

In this general sense, the system created by Stalin was deeply linked internally with the centuries-old tradition of tsarist autocracy (i.e., a type specific kind of absolutism based on Eastern traditions). Functionally speaking—that is, without evaluating the democratic or undemocratic nature of the system or applying any kind of value judgments to it—such a system had certain definite advantages in certain critical historical situations.

These situations can be summarized as follows: The Soviet political system was built in such a way as to enforce one single alternative of action with maximum efficiency— that which corresponded to the momentary will of the power center. In other words, it was capable of concentrating the maximum forces and means in order to achieve a few chosen targets, restrict to a minimum any obstacles which might be encountered, and achieve these goals regardless of the price (economic, social, or cultural) to be paid.

All this may be an advantage in critical situations when only a few selected objectives determine whether a society can or cannot develop in a certain direction. For example, the Soviet political system had functional advantages in wartime and during the speedy industrialization of the USSR (when it created a heavy industrial base from scratch). Though "undemocratic," such a system need not automatically be opposed by strong social forces. So long as the political priorities set by the center correspond somewhat to the interests of strong social groups (classes)—for example, to the national interest in the event of war—such a system is able to muster not only passive loyalty but at times even active and enthusiastic backing from large segments of the society.

But the very characteristics that in specific historical situations create the functional advantages of such a system become, under different circumstances, its defects and fundamental weaknesses. The system becomes incapable of solving basic tasks when it must achieve targets that are not known in advance and have not been formulated by the power center or when it must choose one solution, among several alternatives, that is optimal for the majority.

In such a society, social groups lack the autonomy to be able to govern themselves—that is, to determine their own behavior, needs, and interests as well as the interests and needs of the social entity, by choosing among possible courses of action. The point is not merely that they are bound by the administrative fetters of rigid centralization. What matters above all is that they possess neither the information about nor the feedback from their surroundings that would enable them to seek and find the optimal alternative for themselves. They are the executors of the "central will": Everything else is perceived by the system as an undesirable obstacle, for which reason the system suppresses any other qualities among the people. A society constrained under such a system by its own organization is not, in the end, capable of governing itself from its own power center.[8]

All this must sound very abstract, but I believe it is the only way to express the common denominator underlying the various concrete problems that the radical reform of the Soviet system is intended to solve: insufficient independence among enterprises; inadequate incentives for initiative and for economically efficient operation by producers; shortages of information, and the damage caused by its censorship (both the public managements and state officers have false impressions about this state of affairs); the degeneration of creative activity in science and culture; and the reduction of the law to a mere instrument of state power that is wielded arbitrarily to suppress whatever is considered undesirable.

In the sphere of economic management, Gorbachev's reform policy takes good account of the facts that a specific "braking mechanism" is functioning within the management mechanism, that it is built into the system, and that intensive economic development is possible only if this mechanism is overcome.[9] Such a braking mechanism exists not only in the economy but in the political system as a whole, and it has an impact on all aspects of social life, including the psychology of a people who have grown up under the Soviet system and have known no other. (This, too, is a subject that is beginning to be discussed and written about in the USSR.)[10]

If this braking mechanism is to be overcome in all spheres of society, it must be understood as the reverse side of the basic linkages in the Soviet system that, under different circumstances, were among its advantages. In other words, these system linkages must gradually be replaced by others; and qualitative changes need to be made in such a way that the system will enable society to govern itself. But self-government requires a change in the existing position of all members of society—a change that would enable them to act and decide with the necessary degree of autonomy.

But autonomy cannot be attained through a mere recognition of reality, nor through "correct decisions" of a political nature, nor through changes in just the organizational structures of the management mechanism. It can be achieved only through a transformation of the deeply rooted relations between the regime and society, between the state and civil society, between the individual, social groups, and the social entity. But such a transformation in itself would also be an historical process—one that could not be brought about in one generation alone. Thus a qualitative change (the "revolution" that Gorbachev speaks of) can only begin in the coming decade; it cannot be completed.

Even in the optimal case, whereby Gorbachev's reform concept wins across the board and eliminates its political opponents, a long-term change in the system will be a continuous struggle with the past—and the present is the product of that past. This struggle with the past (the present reality) is politically difficult, complex, and dangerous. The most striking phenomenon of this struggle is the endeavor to come to terms with Stalin's dictatorship. It was in this area, thirty years ago, that Khrushchev began his spectacular criticism of Stalin's "personality cult" and of the crimes perpetrated by his abuse of power. Special attention was naturally given to the measures directed against members of his own Soviet power elite (i.e., to the political trials of communists), especially between 1936 and 1938.

Khrushchev concentrated on Stalin's "objectionable personal qualities," already criticized by Lenin, and on the sphere of criminal repression. This criticism of the Stalinist system alone aroused such strong political opposition that, soon after Khrushchev's downfall, it came to an end. During the long years of Brezhnev's rule there was virtual silence about negative aspects of the past, Stalinist or otherwise.

It appears that at the beginning of his reform offensive, Gorbachev tried to prevent the problem of the conflict with the Stalinist past from intervening too conspicuously and too rapidly in his political endeavors. He must have been afraid that if this conflict became the main issue, it would push into the background the job of making economic, social, and political changes.[11] But two years later it was no longer possible to avoid this problem. The question of the Stalinist past inevitably resurfaced, resulting in slogans about the need for democratization, the restrictions on censorship, and the emphasis on glasnost. Unlike Khrushchev, however, Gorbachev is not trying to limit the issue to Stalin and his personal characteristics. Instead, he has gradually opened discussion about the Soviet period as a development full of contradictions, during which time it would have been possible to proceed in ways other than those followed. It is in this framework that he offered scope for criticism of Stalin—but by no means of Stalin alone. Although it may seem that Stalin is being "absolved," or at least not condemned for his crimes in the same unequivocal terms as under Khrushchev, I am nevertheless of the opinion that Gorbachev's course of action will be better and more consistent in the long run. The main problem for the future is, after all, to make sure that the existence of various possible alternative solutions, the need to choose one of these, and the possibility of making a wrong choice and then correcting it should all be accepted in the public consciousness as necessary and normal facts. And thus Gorbachev's approach to the past—provided it really does lead to a systematic, critical, and democratically conducted discussion about the past—may well open the door to reform more effectively than Khrushchev's earlier criticism of Stalin.

Again, unlike Khrushchev, Gorbachev does not confine his criticism of the Stalin period to mass terror, unjust repression, and criminal abuse of power. He describes all aspects of the system established at the time—from the management of the economy to the political system and culture—as being the products of historical conditions and influences that, while possibly functional under certain conditions, no longer correspond to present-day reality.

Gorbachev's basic formulation that "true" socialism cannot be identified with the historical organization of Soviet society in the 1930s and 1940s[12] is the most profound criticism that has ever been leveled at Stalinism by a Soviet leader. The long years of arguments within the communist movement, in which advocates of certain opinions were not only branded as heretics but in some cases physically liquidated, suddenly come to an end with the admission by the highest Soviet representative that the Soviet system is merely a unique and historically specific case, not a universally binding norm.

At the same time, Gorbachev is judiciously making sure that his criticism of the past does not produce undesirable political consequences in the form of opposition to his reform policy. Indeed, there exist many forces that might be brought together by their determination to prevent a criticism of the past that would "degrade their entire life's work." To some extent this is a generational problem: The generation of people who were politically active under Stalin often feel that any criticism of the system in existence then "devaluates" their life's endeavors.

The populations of the smaller European-bloc states also hold a negative view of the imposition of the Soviet system. This system, they believe, prevented the opportunity for a successful collaboration with West European countries. For Russia, the period between the revolution and the present entailed an incredible rise from a backward agrarian country to a world superpower—hence the often blind acceptance of the system by nationalist-oriented forces in the tradition of Great-Russian chauvinism. This attitude is frequently the only real identification with the system shared by a majority of the population. World War II was the last significant period during which Soviet citizens identified with the system. It was a time when the real choice was not between Stalin's dictatorship and democracy but between survival (under the Stalinist system) and slavery or death.

Given this fact, it is extremely important that Soviet politicians avoid any action that might touch upon the deep sensitivities of the Russian people about their wartime experiences. Gorbachev must therefore manage to criticize the past sixty years of the Soviet system while avoiding the impression that those sixty years were a catastrophe and that the overall balance is a purely negative one. It is only within this context that his statements about the Stalinist past during his speech on the seventieth anniversary of the October Revolution make sense.[13]

A way out of the contradictions inherent in statements such as "on the one hand crimes . . . but on the other successes in construction" can be found neither in Gorbachev's policy as such nor even after a longer period of reform. Thus the reform itself will have to proceed in the face of such contradictions. The relativism of pragmatic approaches and the absolute nature of moral criteria cannot be reconciled or overcome even by a reform policy. These problems can be surmounted only through the long-term evolution of Soviet culture and society—from the political arena.

The inability of the collective consciousness to make a critical analysis of its own past is, of course, a factor that can greatly complicate a radical reform of the system. A certain "pride in one's past" is, in fact, also "pride" in the very features of the system that, no longer capable of ensuring progress today or tomorrow, lead to stagnation and threaten the viability of the system. In the USSR this often applies especially to the mentality that demands authoritarian methods of governing with an "iron fist." (Of course, this "fist" should nevertheless be a "clean hand"—that is, unblemished by Stalin's crimes or by Brezhnev-style corruption.) This mentality, common among very different social groups (not only among the governing elite), is an outright obstacle to system changes in the desired direction—toward a greater autonomy for individuals, a greater measure of democracy, and self-government.

The Soviet past reaches into the present in other ways as well. For example, fundamental interests deriving from the past system are held by certain sections within the existing social structure; and a change in the system would mean a decline in social prestige as well as the loss of advantages and privileges for those groups hitherto favored by the system.

This applies above all to the Soviet bureaucracy, whose very existence is dependent on the kind of system in which power and the decisionmaking process are centralized. In such a system, there are large groups of people whose sole jobs are to pass directives "from above downward" and to supervise their implementation by administrative methods. In a country as huge as the USSR, these people number in the millions. The official figure for the entire Soviet bureaucracy (including the enterprise sphere) is 18 million people. Of these, a large proportion would not be threatened by reform; they would merely have to submit to efficiency criteria and accept jobs in the social division of labor other than those they presently hold. However, the jobs of another segment would evidently become redundant—and even this segment comprises several million people.

Another way in which the past casts its shadow on the present concerns both those who previously have been privileged and others who have not been so. It is clear that, with command management in the economy and in other areas of social life, preference is given to those who follow orders from above, irrespective of their own opinions. Throughout the decades in which the Soviet system has existed, this socio-psychological type has become a representative stratum not only of the power elite but in varying degrees of all social groups, including the workers. The past has created certain deep-rooted habits and attitudes that, by their very nature, have become a hindrance to Gorbachev's reform policy. Official statements still support the notion of egalitarianism (remuneration regardless of performance such that everyone is guaranteed a certain average income and social security) and attempts to secure the maximum from society with a minimum of effort.

But the problem of socio-psychological obstacles to reform goes much deeper; indeed, its roots reach far into Russia's pre-revolutionary past. In Russian history, modernization has been achieved—notably by Peter the Great—through the process of copying selected features of more advanced Western countries while keeping other spheres of social life unchanged. For example, manufacturing, which in the West was connected with the abolition of serfdom and the development of a labor market with free wage laborers, developed in Russia under Peter the Great in a very different manner. His regime forced the serfs (often by physically tying them to instruments of labor or through corporal punishment) to work in manufacturing industries instead of in the fields. Technically a kind of production force was created by this means, but socially it did not lead to the changes that, in the West, accompanied the introduction of the same technology.

Stalin's industrialization process contained similar disparities: Industry, particularly heavy industry, was built, but the social relations that evolved in the West in conjunction with industrialization, developed quite differently in the Soviet Union. Civil society remained essentially passive and poorly structured (or "gelatinous," as Antonio Gramsci describes the civil society in the East), and it was subject to total state control. The division of labor distributed society into groups according to skills required by industrial production, but the social relations among these groups and with the society as a whole—as well as their behavior, conflicts, rivalries, and cooperation—all evolved differently from Western industrial models. A strong argument can be made that, from the technological point of view, the USSR is a modern industrial society; but in the political and social senses it retains powerful elements of its pre-capitalist, semi-feudal past.[14]

Of course, this is true not only of the USSR but also of other Eastern countries. China, for example, is an even more striking case. But whereas the reformers in China have had the courage to admit openly in recent years that many of the country's development problems can be solved only by overcoming the pre-capitalist, feudal remnants of the past, and that China has been grappling with the same problems as other Third World developing countries, in the USSR such candor is not yet possible. True, the USSR is a more advanced country than China and cannot simply declare itself a Third World country. But the problem facing both countries is similar. It involves the coexistence of precapitalist features with an industrialized society that refused, both officially and psychologically, to admit the contradiction. Instead of analysis, we are treated to half-hearted attempts in both countries to defend this discrepancy as "real socialism." All that is "non-capitalist" and "non-Western" has for years been explained simply as "socialist."

In his day Lenin explicitly warned Russian communists against "communist clap-trap," which he believed was as much a threat to socialist development as the bureaucratization of the system. He declared that as soon as the socialist revolution triumphed in one of the advanced Western countries, Russia would once more become a clearly backward country—not only in the technological but also in the "socialist/Soviet" sense of the word.[15] After industrialization was achieved, the official claim was that Lenin's warning no longer applied. But, in truth, Russia's backwardness was overcome neither by industrialization nor by the fact that a socialist revolution had failed to take place in any advanced Western country. The policy of reform inaugurated by Mikhail Gorbachev will have to come to terms, first, with the serious problems that Lenin enunciated so clearly sixty years ago.

Despite the immense political and social significance of Stalin-era discussion, the problem of coming to terms with the past cannot be solved just by identifying it. For a long time to come, the government will likely embellish, rather than criticizing, the past in order to achieve its short-term objectives. From a political standpoint, as Gorbachev declared in one of his speeches, discussion of the past is one of several instruments for implementing the present reform policy.[16] Such discussion, which focuses mainly on the era of Stalin's dictatorship (but, we hope, will in time cover the Khrushchev and Brezhnev eras as well) will certainly excite the interest of the intelligentsia, the politically active segments of the population (such as party members), and the generations who experienced those times.

In any event, the process of overcoming the ingrained and outmoded attitudes that influence the behavior of millions of Soviet citizens, including the least privileged, will be long and difficult. The citizens' relationship to their own political history, as well as the role of individual personalities in that history, poses a somewhat different question. I believe that the consideration of any approach to this question other than a pluralist one is not compatible with the democratization and modernization of Soviet society. Just as Europeans disagree, and will forever disagree, in their assessments of such controversial figures as Marat, Robespierre, and Napoleon, there can never be a uniform judgment in Russia of Lenin, Trotsky, or Stalin. Hence Soviet political history must be studied and analyzed in light of the pragmatic and objective criteria of evaluation that will evolve as new information surfaces. Any attempt to develop a "binding" ideology would not only defeat the entire purpose of this exercise but also signal a return to mindless ideological repression.

The Economy, Politics, and Ideology

The basic problems of the existing Soviet system that have led to the present crisis (or, officially, to "a pre-crisis situation"), and have made a new reform-oriented policy imperative, lie in the economic sphere. A critical analysis of the state of the Soviet economy is still under way, and the Soviet leadership itself repeatedly admits that the situation is worse than it appeared at the beginning of 1985. In his speech to the CPSU Central Committee in February 1988, Gorbachev declared that, not counting the revenue from the sale of oil and natural gas and from alcoholic beverages, the national revenue of the USSR has remained virtually stagnant throughout four five-year plans (i.e., for almost twenty years), and that in the early 1980s it actually decreased. Thus it was critical that the first reform measures should deal with the mechanism of economic management. Indeed, the realization of economic reform is the key to the success of all other proposed reforms.

It has also become clear—as the Soviet leadership has been declaring officially since the beginning of 1987—that economic reform cannot be achieved in the absence of political transformations, democratization, a more informed society, and spirited public involvement in the cause of reform. From this standpoint, political democratization is an essential instrument of economic development, and it must be implemented in conjunction with economic reform.

Gorbachev has recently taken yet another step. At the February session of the CPSU Central Committee in 1988, he presented a report entitled "Revolutionary Restructuring—The Ideology of Revival." Essentially, the report maintains that without a different way of thinking, without a change in the ideology that has prevailed throughout past decades, political or economic reform will be impossible. Three decisive elements of the Soviet system—the mechanism of economic management, the political system, and the official ideology—are mutually interdependent. No radical change can be made in any one of these elements without affecting the other two. Conversely, it is not possible to reform one of these elements in isolation because the other two will not permit such a change.

In a sense, the Stalinist system is dependent on a specific ideological framework that justifies and gives it legitimacy— so long as categorical imperatives, arguments, and an official ideology make it appear the only possible system for the purpose of "building socialism and communism." It was the Stalinist system that devised and elaborated the practice whereby all decisions taken in any sphere of social life— from economy to culture—were subordinated to the ultimate judgment of the official ideology. And if something failed to be justified in the eyes of the official ideological system, it could be eliminated from social life—by force, if necessary. This approach was applied to all spheres, from market relations in the economy to artistic trends that were contrary to "socialist realism." In short, the official ideology became a linchpin for the whole system.

Although the decisive role in facilitating the very existence of the system was naturally played by economic, social, and power-political relations, in the final analysis all of these relations were in one way or another subjected to the official ideology. Only those trends that official ideology recognized as being "socialist and communist" could be practised and developed in these relations. Or, to put it more precisely, the trends not sanctioned by ideology could exist only semilegally or illegally, and could function only in a concealed and hence distorted way. This applied to the economy as well as to the culture: In the economy, ideologically unsanctioned market mechanisms existed as a "second economy" (i.e., a semilegal or illegal market of labor and commodities, or a "black market" as in a wartime economy); in the culture, meanwhile, old values, ideological attitudes, and religious beliefs dating back to pre-Stalinist days form an effective counter-culture.

In a Stalinist-type system, just as in medieval theocratic systems, people were arrested and even executed on the grounds of "ideological deviations" (i.e., of views conflicting with the official ideological system). For many years these practices created a climate of fear that not only prevented the dissemination of views contrary to official ideology but also ensured that such views did not even arise in the minds of the majority of people.

Under these circumstances, the mutual dependence of the three elements in the Soviet system—the mechanism of economic management, the political system, and the official ideology—becomes a vicious circle in which one element blocks the others and all three hinder the development of fundamental change.

Although basic economic problems are soluble, they can be tackled only by modifying the official ideology. For example, in the process of eliminating the methods of a command economy, in which enterprises receive the targets and limits of their economic activity in the form of detailed plan indices, the awareness that administrative methods of command are the main cause of stagnation, and of the inability of the Soviet economy to turn to intensive growth, does not lead to a solution. Ideological innovation is essential: Official ideology must explain that different methods of management—based on the use of economic stimuli and, to some extent, market mechanisms—are not anti-socialist; on the contrary, they are compatible with the "building of socialism and communism."

In the absence of substantial ideological innovations, reform in the USSR cannot ultimately succeed, in either the economic or political sphere. Hence the "struggle against dogmatism" (i.e., against attempts to preserve the ideological system in its present form) is of key importance. The new Soviet leadership must see the question of "dogmatism" not in a purely theoretical vein but as a problem that involves the interests of certain segments of the ruling bureaucracy who are trying to retain their present positions and privileges.[17]

At this point, no innovation can take place in official Soviet ideology—except as an attempt at a new interpretation of the views of Marx and, more particularly, of Lenin as compared to the interpretation canonized by Stalin. It is unrealistic to suppose that one can simply discard the present (Stalinist) ideological system, begin to think pragmatically, and test empirically all the theses and views that govern practical action. Such as approach would not constitute a reform of the existing system; neither would they be a "revolution from above," as they would lead to the destruction of the existing system. If this system is to undergo long-term qualitative changes without upheaval, change must begin with gradual reforms and innovations of the ideological system, not with the destruction of that system.

The decisive new factor in this scenario is the recognition that even within the framework of communist ideology, a solution can and must be sought by assessing various possibilities; that a "socialist pluralism of views"[18] is not only possible but absolutely essential; and that during certain turning points in history, it is necessary to admit "that our entire perception of socialism has been changed" (as Lenin remarked about his New Economic Policy). Given the appeal of Lenin's pragmatic approach to problem solving (which is shared by Gorbachev), it should be possible to eliminate the canonized ideological "precepts" that have been the touchstone of Soviet policy since Stalin.

This pragmatic approach has so far been most evident in the sphere of foreign policy: Here the "new political thinking," as it is officially called, has become the basis of changes in political action (see Chapter 3). A similar course of events is essential also in the sphere of internal policy. And in this respect developments in the USSR are still only just beginning.

The 19th All-Union CPSU Conference in June 1988 greatly strengthened the position of the forces linked with the reform ideology. As the Conference demonstrated, there is no one in either the ruling party or the bureaucracy capable of advancing an alternative to Gorbachev's policies. This is not to say, of course, that everyone is an advocate of the current reform program; nor is there a united view about the future among them. (This conclusion can be inferred from the Conference speeches and from the responses—as well as the facial expressions—of many participants.) But no real political opposition to Gorbachev's reform—not even an overall conservative alternative—has emerged.

Gorbachev repeatedly stated at the Conference that the irreversibility of perestroika is not yet guaranteed. But it has become clear since the Conference that his position is not threatened for the foreseeable future, and that his program will be more than just a short-lived episode. Those who have simply been waiting to see if Gorbachev will "hold out" will thus have to decide definitely for or against his policy. On the one hand, we can expect to see both growing support for perestroika within the political power apparatus among those who are now beginning to think it is winning and will be good for their careers, and gradually mounting support from below in the form of spontaneous pressure from various social forces and groups. On the other hand, those who have decided that "enough is enough," that the reform movement has reached the limits of what they are willing to tolerate, will be forced to take more offensive action. The next two years or so (i.e., up to the pre-congress period in 1989 and 1990) will be critical. Then the 28th Congress of the CPSU will be held. Given that upheavals (insofar as they happen in Soviet politics) take place not at the congresses but between congresses, when they are in preparation (when members of the winning political trend are elected as delegates), the necessary conflict over the fate of perestroika will be fought out roughly one year prior to the coming congress. Matters of personnel are far from being the only issues, but they will certainly play a part.

I do not share the view that the reform program would benefit at present from an open conflict between the radical and conservative wings in the leadership (usually represented as a latent conflict when Gorbachev and Ligachev). On the contrary, I think that a positive feature of the Soviet situation is that a split has not occurred in the leadership, which has managed thus far, more or less democratically, to maintain representation from the various trends that exist within the Communist party, in the power elite as a social stratum, and in society at large. Simply to prevent the opinions that Ligachev is usually taken to symbolize from being voiced either in the party leadership or in public statements would be to suppress a strong trend that would continue to exist. It could become the channel in which variously motivated anti-reform efforts could ultimately join together under the surface to form a strong and dangerous force capable of threatening the reform movement itself. So long as this trend finds itself represented in the official structures, it will not escape democratic encounters—

at least to the extent that democratic rules are actually applied within the official structures.

It is obviously necessary for the success of the reform that the radical trend should show strength and the conservative trend should grow weaker, in both the party and the state leaderships. But that can happen only when the radical supporters of reform have gained a real majority among the public, within the power elite, and among Communist party members. Such a majority would involve a more difficult, complex, and long-term process than a fight for top posts resulting in the ousting of conservative representatives from positions in the public view without altering their grass-roots support. Such a process could weaken—even threaten—the reform, as happened toward the end of Khrushchev's government and to some extent also during the Prague Spring in Czechoslovakia.

On the home front during the next phase of the reform, ideological innovation ("new thinking") will see ideology employed as an effective instrument for modernizing the Soviet system, both economically and politically. Yet we cannot expect official Soviet ideology to abandon either its declared objectives (the building of communism) or its traditional sources (especially Lenin's ideas). The idea that this is what can be expected from the reform movement is among the unrealistic notions accepted in the West.

For the foreseeable future, innovation in Soviet ideology may, in fact, consist of finding a new interpretation of what is and what is not "socialist" (or, possibly, what serves and what does not serve the "building of communism"). This interpretation will thus have a common denominator: Everything that proves to be (and will continue to prove to be) necessary for the transition from extensive to intensive economic growth will be newly interpreted as "socialist."

These emerging Soviet concepts may strike left wingers in the West either as totally irrelevant to their experience or as geared toward the pragmatic approaches to basic problems of efficiency and progress that face any industrialized state. It is probable, therefore, that despite the removal of a whole series of barriers which decades of Stalinist ideology and practice have erected between Western socialist thinking and Soviet practice, not even the new Soviet reform policy will be able in the near future to find a common ideological language with Western socialist and left-wing forces.

Probably only in the long term—if the USSR really achieves its planned modernization and reaches a stage of industrial development comparable to the present degree of development in the West (in the technical but also the sociopolitical sense)—can we expect to see the new ideology having to tackle the kinds of questions that the Western left is facing today (e.g., the limits of economic growth, the priority of ecological problems, preference for leisure time over the rise of material standards, and the emancipation of different social groups, especially women). But in the current phase of development, these and similar problems will not be the crucial issues of ideological innovation.

Perhaps the most important challenge facing the USSR today is to achieve a change in thinking whereby socialism becomes identified in the public consciousness with an efficient society and not with the principle of minimum security regardless of performance. In Soviet ideological terminology, the principle of remuneration according to the quantity, quality, and—above all—the end effect of labor must be made to apply, without exception, to all social strata (including the ruling bureaucracy). Currently this is the main theme in Gorbachev's speeches when he is dealing with the question of social justice under socialism—a justice that is served by the principle of remuneration according to performance.

It is over this issue that the major battle is being waged in the USSR today against the existing practice, which declares as "socialist principles" those pre-capitalist (semi-feudal) features of Soviet society that include privileges based on caste and class, minimum social security regardless of performance (ensured by the state or "socialist enterprises" in place of the extended family), the tendency towards egalitarianism as the ideal of social justice, and so on.

The second fundamental problem confronting the emerging ideology is how to come to terms with the role of the market in a socialist economy. Current ideology, which in many ways is based on pre-capitalist traditions, saw the market, its accompanying competitive relationships, bankruptcy, and, most of all, the possibility of making a profit (not sanctioned in advance) as being unacceptable in principle to relations between socialist enterprises. Socialism envisaged a command economy (if possible, from a single center) in which the decisionmaking center made all production decisions and posed the conditions governing distribution, the preference to be given to various products, and so forth. This form of economic management has inevitably led to the present economic stagnation. The way out of the crisis lies in an entirely different treatment of the relationship between the market and the economic plan—and the precondition for this is to create in the Soviet mind a different ideological concept about the significance of the market.

The third problem of fundamental significance is the ideological concept of the social needs and interests of Soviet society. Heretofore official ideology has proceeded from the principle that it was the governing center—in practice, the center of political power (i.e., the leadership of "party and state"—that determined social policy; the center then laid down the priorities for the various goals to be attained. Anything that ran counter to the achievement of these few objectives inevitably appeared as disruptive, and the center then attempted to suppress all such elements. Underlying this concept was the assumption that society was an object governed by one of its parts (its "vanguard") that alone had the ability to perceive the interests of the community.

But if the USSR is to modernize in the economic, social, and political spheres (as Gorbachev has outlined in various documents), the new approach must be based on the concept of society as an organism capable of governing itself.[19] Self-government requires that all the basic social entities (from large social groups such as nations and classes, to smaller groups created by the division of labor, to the individual citizen) have sufficient decisionmaking autonomy in the economic, social, and political systems. Toward this end, the administrative barriers to autonomous behavior created by all these social entities would have to be removed; but even more important, the state would have to provide a de facto prerequisite for this autonomy—namely, freedom of information. Only a society that is fully informed is able to govern itself by democratic methods—that is, by the confrontation of different points of view, such that the will of the social majority can ultimately be ascertained. To demonstrate by ideological arguments that this (and not "government by an omniscient center") is the socialist way will be one of Gorbachev's essential tasks.[20]

As long as "new thinking" on these three basic issues—the principle of a performance-based society, an adequate role for the market in the economy, and the possibility for social entities to act autonomously—is not generally accepted, it will be impossible to carry out either an economic or a political reform in the USSR. The process of ideological innovation concerning these issues will be lengthy and full of contradictions; there will be defeats as well as victories.

On the surface these three ideological issues may seem abstract. In reality, ideological innovation involves modifying the position of entire social groups in Soviet society, often against their interests.

The first two issues—the principle of performance and the role of the market—affect the economy in particular. But they also affect the privileges and rank of different groups (especially but not exclusively of the bureaucracy). They involve the emergence of unemployment on the one hand and the conspicuous enrichment of certain groups on the other. The third—social autonomy—concerns both the economy (mainly the position of enterprise) and the political system. Social groups and individuals must resolve their differences within a context in which the state guarantees their autonomy and freedom of expression. This situation cannot fail to give rise to serious conflicts in a society which has been developing over decades according to vastly different principles, and which even in centuries of history has no traditions on which to draw in solving the problems posed by the need to modernize and restructure the existing system.

These tasks, including the indispensable innovation of official ideology, cannot be accomplished by any one section of Soviet society. A reform of the system thus cannot be the job exclusively of the so-called technocracy, for the technocracy is not capable of bringing about ideological innovation. In my view it is unrealistic to believe that "pressure from below" against the official political structure—and, more particularly, against the monopoly of the ruling Communist party—could enforce fundamental changes. The tasks that I have mentioned can be fulfilled in Soviet society (if they can be fulfilled at all) only if the long-term reform, both "from above" and "from below," takes place in an incremental way: Any effort to bring about the speedy destruction of the existing economic and political system would be extremely dangerous.

A model cannot be found in the behavior of societies such as Poland, Hungary, or Czechoslovakia. Despite many differences, the reform movements in these countries have had one thing in common: There existed in the social consciousness (in the memory of society), at least in general terms, a vision of a different model for the social system, and this vision provided a precedent for spontaneous sociopolitical activities. Such a situation does not exist in the USSR; on the contrary, pressure "from below" is often conservative and will require a long-term process before the idea of anything other than an authoritarian model for the sociopolitical system can emerge. In short, a solution will have to be sought both "from above" and "from below."

That is why the problem of ideological innovation is unavoidable. The idea, common in the West, that the official ideology carries no great weight in the USSR, because no one really believes in "communism," is an extreme simplification. True, objective opinion polls would likely show that, for the great majority of Soviet citizens the official ideology is no more than a ritual—and, specifically, a ritual that does not determine their personal behavior, which is decided by more genuinely operative sets of values and ideas.

This is not to say that a system change can occur without ideological innovation. For one thing, official ideology does make a strong impact on social consciousness—because it accepts as "socialism" a distorted reality, sanctioned by ideology. This reality is in jeopardy and, hence, must change. Furthermore, the official ideology is the only system by which the power elite conceives of reality, of the connections among the economy, politics, and social life, between domestic and foreign policy, and so on. Just as it is impossible to exchange in one stroke the existing power elite of society for another, it is equally impossible to get rid of the ideology through which this elite perceives both the social reality and its own functions.

There is a way out of the vicious circle of interdependence among the economy, politics, and ideology, but this way out can be achieved only through ideological innovation.

2 / How Can the Political Institutions in the USSR Be Reformed?

The substantial changes that have taken place in the USSR in recent years are essentially changes in the political atmosphere, changes in the methods and style of policy-making. This is also true of the policy of glasnost: Not one of the institutions that in the past controlled the censorship of published information has yet been abolished. Nevertheless, a "behavioral" change has occurred: for the most part, these institutions no longer interfere in the activities of the mass media and in the dissemination of information. Apart from the emergence of certain new associations, clubs, and smaller organizations—those that somehow survived in the shade of semilegality or illegality—the institutional political system of the USSR has thus far remained virtually unchanged by the reform policy. Only in economic management has more evident reorganization occurred: Certain old organizational forms have disappeared and new ones have been created. But this reorganization has no significance for the fundamental structure of the political system.

Some Westerners have thus concluded that the reform of the political system has not even begun; that it will be possible to speak of a political reform only when more fundamental changes have been made, such as changes in the position and role of existing institutions, the disappearance of some of them, and the simultaneous emergence and functioning of new institutions. In my opinion, however, this concept would not be quite correct. I agree that as long as a new relationship between society and the regime are not institutionally founded and guaranteed, the irreversibility of the reforms cannot be postulated; merely temporary, they will depend on the whims of the Soviet leadership. But I also believe that a number of qualitative changes in the Soviet political system can be implemented within the existing institutions by means of gradual reforms of these institutions and their mutual relationships. Genuine radical reform, (i.e., a change of the system) requires that new institutions be created, even over the long term.

The main question to be resolved is this: How can the institutions of the political system (those of the future as well as the present) become responsive to different social needs and interests, such that political decisionmaking does not defy the will of the majority? This question can be tackled within the framework of existing institutional systems, above and beyond that of the parliamentary-type pluralist democracy in the Western tradition. But certain principles must be respected in the process—namely, the principles that provide for an adequate measure of control by society over the activities of bodies in which power is concentrated.

It is in this area that the existing practice of the Soviet political system must be changed; this very control was lacking in the Stalinist system, and it remains utterly inadequate in the USSR to this day. How are the political institutions in the USSR to be reformed so as to effect a true democratic decisionmaking process? In this chapter I shall try to give a brief answer.

The Role of the Communist Party in the Reform of the Soviet System

The Communist party is the key institution of the entire Soviet political system. To understand the party's significant role in Soviet society, we must know something of its historical development. An abundance of literature, both apologetic and critical, exists on this subject. But in this study I must confine myself to a few brief remarks.

The origin of the monopolistic position of the Communist party in the Soviet system, as well as the complex relationships within the party, can be understood only within the historical context of the Russian Revolution. This point was conceded quite openly not only by Lenin but by Stalin as well.[21] It is essential to remember that the program of the socialist revolution as conceived by the Bolsheviks had a very narrow social base.[22] For the Communist party the main problem soon became one of maintaining control over events and developments that did not correspond to its program. Thus, after the seizure of power, the party soon developed an apparatus bent on exerting total control over the entire government, the state, the economy, various public organizations, and individual movement. Especially in rural areas, events moved "spontaneously": Having nothing in common with the communist program, they led to the expansion of private small-scale production and a market economy.

Various elite groups—from civil servants to economists and the officer corps—were hostile to the communist revolutionary policy. The party therefore attempted to place these groups under the control of politically loyal plenipotentiaries—the so-called commissars. This system of commissars and the creation of various other "extraordinary and all-powerful" commissions led to the establishment of a new politically committed communist apparatus over and above the "normal" governing machinery. This apparatus was endowed with absolute power and destined to enforce "the policy of the party" by any means, including terror.

As this process developed, it was subjected to criticism within the European communist and labor movements and, to some extent, even in Soviet Russia.[23] The main contention of the critics—namely, that the dictatorship of the proletariat was being replaced in the name of the proletariat by the dictatorship of the party over society (including the working class)—was firmly rejected by Stalin. Under his leadership, the process of transforming the party into an apparatus of control advanced even further: De facto centers of absolute power emerged within the party, capable of deciding on anything and everything, and accountable to no one except their own hierarchy. The Communist party itself evolved into a peculiar organization that to some extent merged with various segments of the pre-revolutionary elite— namely, the state administration, the army, the police, and the economic sector.

In the years of Stalin's dictatorship—from the 1930s to the 1950s—the situation was no longer post-revolutionary; there was no opposition and thus no need to create a network of commissars. Under Stalin, many important professional positions required party membership. Appointments to a whole range of top posts were made by party bodies. (The lists of offices that required party approval are traditionally known as *nomenklatura* in the USSR; hence the term *nomenclature,* meaning social group, is used for all those holding such offices.) Nomenclature embraces an extremely wide range of socio-professional offices—from the highest position in the state administration or the economy down to the manager of a factory, a hospital, or even a school.

This system of party control over all management personnel exists to this day. Although the party demands that only certain posts be filled by its members, it nevertheless sees itself as totally responsible for the administration of the state. Available statistics do not give us a picture of the proportion of party members who hold positions of power and management. It is my guess that this amounts to almost 30 percent—if we include all management posts, from the lowest to the highest in both the political and economic spheres. Of course, this is not to say that the party in the Soviet system is identical with the social stratum of the power elite: Party members are recruited from various social strata. The reality is that, to an important extent, the party apparatus overlaps with the administration. This situation has had serious consequences. Unfortunately, official Soviet ideology still views the party as the "vanguard of the Soviet people" that unites the "most conscious members of the working class, collective farmers and the intelligentsia" (as formulated in the 1986 CPSU statutes).

Since the Stalin era, official ideology has asserted that the party, as the "vanguard of the people," should be guaranteed the "leading role" in the Soviet system. Yet this general principle can have different interpretations. In its classical Stalinist form, it had two meanings: First, as I have pointed out, the power elite belonged to the party and was totally dependent on it. Second, all decisions, in whatever sphere of social life (including policy, the economy, the judiciary, and culture) were subject in principle to the approval of the Party apparatus. Of course, the party did not make every decision at every level; on important matters, however, its opinion was decisive.

This principle had two fundamental consequences for the Stalinist political system. On the one hand, the party apparatus gradually merged with that of both the state and the economy. This occurred because as the party increased its involvement in the state, economic, and cultural spheres, nonparty managers and bureaucrats tended to seek party approbation in advance for their policies.

On the other hand, two different governing structures arose within the political system in all spheres of social life—from politics and the economy to culture. The official, visible structure was regulated by the Constitution and by legal norms that also stipulated the specific powers of their individual components, their mutual relations, and their responsibilities. The unofficial structure, though hidden, developed from the merging of the party with the official governing apparatus. It was completely unregulated. It had no concept of the principles of division of labor and mutual control of power within the overall power structure. The levels of responsibility, too, were determined by the hierarchy of party-power centers. In actual fact, a system of power centers and their apparatuses emerged outside the constitutional and legal system. They are by their very nature centers of absolute power (at the local, district, and national levels).

These centers of absolute power originated within the Communist party. Formally we can say that they are primarily the presidiums and secretariats of party committees at various levels. The highest of these, the Presidium (known also as the Politburo) and the Secretariat of the Central Committee, create a collective absolute ruler (dictator) for the whole state. The internal situation within this body determines the extent to which the classical one-man dictatorship (typical especially of the Stalin period) can develop in this model.

These centers of absolute power and the apparatuses connected with them make decisions concerning any question regardless of the Constitution, the legal code, the principles of the division of labor, and the responsibilities of individual management bodies. As noted, not all decisions are discussed in the relevant center of absolute power. But when an issue arises in such a center (for example, the Politburo), the body might make a decision about the economic plan, foreign policy, appointments to various posts (either in accordance with the "nomenclature" or in disregard of it), penal policy as a whole, or even individual court verdicts. Such decisions are then binding on all other bodies of the governing system.

In this system the principle of the "leading role of the party" means that nothing may be decided by a ruling body against the will of the party power centers. Whenever a decision contrary to the interests of the party is taken, the power centers of the party are able to change it or declare it null and void.

That decisions by these centers do not remain mere wishes but are actually implemented (at least where this can be ensured by administrative methods) is made possible by the fact that all members of the power elite—from the prime minister or the district judge to the manager of a factory or a headmaster—are members of the Communist party. They are therefore bound by internal party discipline, and, even more important, they depend on party power centers for their livelihood.

These are the most obvious features characterizing the Communist party's monopolistic role in the Soviet (Stalinist) type system, but the significance of the party cannot be reduced to them alone. The party is not a unique political institution; it also serves to link the power elite of the state with all classes of Soviet society. The party is a special kind of sociopolitical organism; within its framework, authority is linked with the interests of certain social groups in a very peculiar way.

As pointed out earlier, the majority of party members (about 66 percent) are not members of the power elite. About 40 percent of this membership belong to the party in order to advance their professional careers, and because they enjoy certain advantages. This applies to a whole series of socially privileged people whose professions require specialized qualifications (such as a technical or university education)—from the technical intelligentsia to scientists, teachers, doctors, and journalists. In the Soviet system, membership in the party is, if not a condition, then at least an advantage in advancing one's professional career.

In my opinion, the immense growth in the number of party members—from just under 7 million at the time of Stalin's death (in 1953) to roughly 20 million today—can be explained by the expansion of the social strata for whom skilled work and, hence, more privileged professions are linked with membership in the party. The remaining members—just over 25 percent—consist of workers, collective farmers, and other nonprivileged social groups.

There is no doubt that membership in the party offers certain advantages—even to members who are workers. At the least, a useful political status is assured. Party members have greater opportunities for political influence on the "power sphere" than nonmembers. Overall, therefore, the party members are more in tune with the existing economic, social, and political system than are nonparty citizens.

Today, roughly every tenth adult in the USSR is a member of the party. A wide range of social interests and viewpoints have thus been introduced into the party—interests and viewpoints that go far beyond those of the power apparatus. This is one of the most significant changes to have occurred since Stalin's dictatorship. Back then, the range of social interests represented within the party was much smaller, and the predominance of the views held by the power apparatus (including the ideological apparatus) was unquestionable.

As a consequence, a process has developed in the party that, by degrees, could strengthen the influence on political decisionmaking of those social needs and interests that are represented within the party, yet are not identical with the narrow interests of the power elite as such, nor of the power apparatus that is integrated in the party as well. Thus the crucial question is whether there exists (or can develop) inside the party the chance that effective control over the apparatus of power and government may be exerted by other social forces—or whether, on the contrary, the interests of all social forces in the party are largely subordinated to the position of the power apparatus and the power elite connected with it. In other words, can the party—under Soviet conditions—become an institution whose democratization may be the starting point for democratizing the entire political system?

In the Soviet system, the party resembles a kind of sieve that lets through only those social interests and needs able to influence (legally and with political effect) the process of decisionmaking. If the party is unaffected by these interests and needs, the political system regards them as quite undesirable—as obstacles, possibly even as "hostile forces"—and suppresses them by every means.

Conflicts about which (and to what degree) social interests are to exert an influence within the party represent an ever-present tendency. After all, the question has always been whether the party as a social organism will be subordinated to the party as a power apparatus, or vice versa. In the past, the former alternative has always won the upper hand, while the latter has remained a program and a hope. The policy of "restructuring" will sooner or later have to fight a decisive battle in behalf of the latter alternative.

As with the entire political system of the USSR, the fact that the party is able to enforce a uniform will, and concentrate all its forces and means on achieving a central decision, once adopted, has for many decades been considered fundamentally important. In theory, this type of decisionmaking occurs on the basis of Lenin's principle of democratic centralism: Democratic discussion before the adoption of a decision is meant to be combined with strict discipline, which must be observed by all party members once the decision has been adopted; and the democratic and autocratic principles should achieve a balance.

In practice, however, this theoretically assumed balance has an unexpected result. There have been long periods in the history of the party during which no democratic discussion has taken place prior to the adoption of a decision. But even majority support for a decision disguises the fact that it has been carried by a majority and the illusion is created that the resolution reflects the opinion of everyone without exception. A situation where there is absolutely no conflict of views, as if just one alternative course existed, is seen as an ideal state of affairs. Party members are expected not to express their differing views, and to act in accordance with a resolution even if they have doubts about its correctness.

In certain very exceptional situations this may be an advantage in an organization—particularly during the preparation for an uprising, in a war situation, or during some other extreme conflict where any alternative course has to be suppressed, liquidated, or prevented. But in all other situations it is a shortcoming. Even in the pursuit of one general objective—for example, the program of a political party—there are always several possible alternatives for action that are not mutually exclusive and shouldn't cancel each other out if the outcome is not to be stagnation rather than development or diversity.

Insofar as organizations, officials, and members in the party tend to be judged mainly on the basis of how far they are capable of carrying out a resolution regardless of their own views, the major criterion is a demand not for a reasoned unity but for obedience to the authority of the center. Independent thinking and judgment by party members based on their own common sense and conscience carry little weight compared to the "collective will and wisdom of the party," conveyed in instructions from its center and apparatus.

Undemocratic and authoritarian methods and working habits prevail within the party. Precedence is given to a particular psychological type of official and party member. People willing to obey instructions from authoritarian apparatuses irrespective of their own views tend to prevail, whereas those who take a critical view of situations and of individual actions according to their own understanding and conscience are pushed into the background, silenced, and often even driven out of the party.

At the outset, however, no innovation can be anything but a minority initiative. As long as the right to hold minority views is denied, those people with a spirit of initiative and innovation will always be the ones to suffer. Not even the majority will find favor—only the average individuals who are capable of adapting at all times and to anything.

Given these characteristics can the party be transformed from an instrument of absolute power over society into an instrument of democratization? Many authors in the West have replied to this question in the negative: So long as the monopoly position of a single party remains, and so long as this party is the present Communist party, the road toward political democracy in the USSR is closed. Most of these authors do not think that development could, in practice, create other political parties that would compete in elections with the Communist party and thus win a share in the exercise of power (possibly even a decisive share). They are therefore pessimistic about the prospects for democratizing the Soviet system. They believe that reforms cannot change much in the present nature of the system; indeed, they would make no more than certain "cosmetic adjustments" to an essentially untouched system of absolute power and total control of society.

I do not share this pessimistic view. Qualitative changes in the system *are* possible, I believe; and democratization can be implemented even with the existence of one single political party. But the course of this democratization will naturally be full of conflicts, and it will differ from the development of the Western (parliamentary) type of political system as well as from the original ideological concept of Lenin's "republic of councils (soviets)" as a democratic system of the nonparliamentary type.

Briefly, and therefore in simplified terms, I see the development of the Communist party in the Soviet system as taking the following directions. First of all, we must consider how relations develop within the party itself. In this connection, democratization may mean that the party as an apparatus of power will be subjected to increasing control by the party as a social body. In practice, this means that the numerical minority of party members who, in a social sense, belong to the power elite (i.e., who make up the power apparatus) can be controlled effectively and called upon to account for their actions; they may also be given binding political directives by the majority who, again in a social sense, belong to groups or sections other than the power elite.

Even if this objective were to be attained, Soviet society as a whole would not be democratized. What would be established, however, is a process in which the power elite as a special social section would have to learn to respect fundamental democratic rules. This process, of course, is an exceptionally important one. I believe that no society (including the Soviet system) is able to administer itself democratically if its own power elites are not capable of adapting to democratic habits.

The Stalinist system created a power elite that was based on an entirely undemocratic, semifeudal hierarchical structure. At its peak there was an absolute ruler, accountable to no one, to whom all other holders of power—those who held the key positions in the governing process and those whose livelihood depended on him—submitted like vassals. The fundamental criterion of success within this elite was obedience to instructions from above. Responsibility to the membership of the party or to one's electorate was a purely formal matter that in no way was decisive for the careers or downfalls of individual officials in the governing system.

Only insofar as this situation gradually changes (and, indeed, a number of practical steps have already been taken in this direction) will there be an advance in the direction of possible democratic reform. Only when the principle of judging by performance is applied within the power elite itself (instead of the existing principle of obedience) will a different social type start to be given preference. That is, a move from the executor of orders to the managerial type will take place. Of course, such a move in itself is not democratization, not even within the power elite; but it is a precondition. For, in the first place, the individual members of this group need to take responsibility for the results of their actions; only then can the question be put as to whom they are accountable. Yet it is from this quite basic level, and not at higher levels of development, that the process of democratization must start in the USSR.

It is possible to begin teaching the power elite to observe the elementary rules of democratic relations among themselves, even under the regime of a single political party, when that party itself is an organization of the power elite. I believe that the USSR is moving in this direction in three important respects.

1. A fight is being carried on against corruption, nepotism, and anything else that creates in the eyes of the public the image of the official (communist) bureaucrat as inefficient, incompetent, and impersonal. Some of the privileges of the power elite are being either abolished or tied to performance.

In short, an endeavour is being made to renew the shaken confidence of the majority of the population, especially the key social groups and generations, in the party's ability to change the long-standing order of things, including conditions within the party.

2. Within the party, and with its help, a start has been made to overcome the ossified ideology that is no longer capable of being an instrument for understanding the contemporary social reality in either the USSR or the rest of the world.

3. These first steps have been taken toward applying democratic principles within the party itself, especially in elections to some party posts (i.e., secret elections with several candidates), in inner-party criticism, and so on. Party bodies and officials are now subject to the law in their work. The immunity of party officials (especially the top people), frequently granted in the past even in relation to the criminal law, is now explicitly rejected and condemned. The policy of glasnost is progressively being promoted within the party as well, resulting in public criticism at party meetings and in the press. Moreover, self-confidence seems to be slowly growing among the ordinary party members who do not belong to the social stratum of the power elite. As these people gain positive experience, their actual involvement in the process of party democratization will also increase.

Despite these advances, however, the key problems that must be dealt with, if the Soviet political system is to undergo radical democratization, remain more or less unaffected. These problems are connected with the process that led to the merging of party and state, with the de facto domination within the party by the section of the membership that is identical in the social sense to the power elite, and with the formation of a vast bureaucratic apparatus holding absolute sway over the party as a whole.

Gorbachev touched on these key problems (as yet he has *only* touched on them) when, in an unpublished discussion with intellectuals, he expressed the thought that since no opposition party exists in the USSR, the functions of such a party need to be provided in other ways—both through criticism within the Communist party and through other forms of effective criticism.[24]

To my mind, the main requirement for a process that would lead to a satisfactory solution of these key problems is the progressive separation of the state from the mechanism of economic management, in terms of both content and personnel. In other words, party bodies should not decide about matters within the competence of other authorities; and the practice whereby representatives of other authorities are automatically members of party bodies, and leading positions are filled under the "nomenclature procedure", must cease. (That is, the top people in all spheres must no longer be dependent for their jobs on party approval.) In my view, such a process is possible, but it will be extremely difficult; although it would not involve the disappearance of the power elite as a social group (its existence depends both on the division of labor and on the social contradications inherent in the society), it would mean a qualitative change in the internal structure, in the process of formation and social stabilization. But if the principles of a performance-based society are really to prevail and the pre-capitalist (caste-status) elements in Soviet society are to be eliminated, such a development is necessary.

The outcome, in the long term, would have to be the disappearance of the centers of absolute power based in the party that make arbitrary decisions on any question without regard to division of labor, competence, and accountability. In that case the party authorities could become bodies for setting political priorities and general concepts, to be implemented through the work of the party as a social organism, rather than through administrative orders that are binding for the entire management system, the state, the economic bodies, various social organizations, and the institutions.

Based on the number of principles already formulated by the new leadership, it appears that the need to separate "party from state" has been recognized, along with the need for party authorities to relinquish absolute power and abandon the command methods for putting across the "party line." But let us not forget that, in general terms, this has always been recognized; Stalin raged against "administrative methods" even though he created an entire system ensuring their unconditional dominance.

Within the party itself, other guarantees are needed in this respect, in addition to the formulation of the appropriate line of policy. Above all, a different approach would have to be taken to the position of the professional (paid) party apparatus. It would have to be as small as possible, concerned not with controlling the work of the apparatus of state and economic affairs but with organizing and providing practical help for the everyday political activity of party officials and members. An important step in this direction was made by the plenary session of the Central Committee on 30 September 1988.[25] All the departments in the Central Committee apparatus that previously supervised economic affairs, mirroring the structure of the state economic departments, have simply been disbanded. Their staff have been drafted into the ministries. The political apparatus of the Central Committee will now be organized to match six newly formed commissions. These are to cover the most important areas of party policy (inner-party affairs and personnel, foreign affairs, ideology, economic and social policies, agriculture, and law). The commissions' work is to be concerned with preparing material for decision by the Politburo and Central Committee, and producing the necessary political analyses. The job of this restructured apparatus is to prepare material, but not to supervise the departments of state or other organizations. But the actual tasks and composition of the commissions, on which much depends, are not yet known.

Other radical ideas about the party apparatus have been voiced: for instance, that the staff themselves should be elected by party members and made accountable to them and that they should hold their posts for limited terms (that would imply that the principle of rotation should also apply to paid staff).[26]

A second important guarantee against antidemocratic tendencies within the party needs to be firmly established. This guarantee concerns the right for a minority to maintain its view even after a decision has been taken with which it disagrees in part or in full—and to be able to demand, within a certain time, a new decision on the disputed question. Indeed, without the right of minorities to exist and to criticize, fundamental criticism could not really develop and decisionmaking would always involve a choice among alternatives rather than simple agreement or disagreement with a single proposal. However, the right of minorities to exist need not mean that the party would be torn by factional struggles. So-called factions are groups that, in opposing decisions adopted by the party, act outside its ranks and mobilize political forces against its decisions; they are not identical with minority views operating within the party.[27]

It is difficult to say today when and how radically such changes will be carried out in the Communist party. They are nevertheless basically in line with the general trend toward the "return to Lenin"—because during Lenin's lifetime, discussion was not only possible within the party, it was the rule.

Of course, if a Communist party in the Soviet system, where it remains the only political party, is really to achieve "separation from the state" in the sense indicated, one cannot expect everything to depend on the goodwill and correct methods of communists and party officials alone. If the system as a whole is to be truly democratized, the Communist party must place itself in a position within the system such that it is impracticable to remain (or return) as a holder of absolute power not subject to democratic control.

Goodwill alone, then, is not enough to prevent society from being subordinated once more to centers of absolute power and to total control of all movement in society. Other agencies (the state and its elected bodies, enterprises and economic organizations, interest groups, and so on) must have sufficient authority to be able to act autonomously without instructions from Party organizations and officialdom to make decisions, take certain steps, and reject others.

In short, democratization is possible with a single political party so long as its position does not develop into a monopoly of exclusive power in the process of political decisionmaking. Guarantees against such a monopoly must be provided not only in the party but also outside it. Also needed are agencies with sufficient autonomy to prevent the party from developing in this way.

A practical step in this direction would be the subordination of party organizations (and officials) to the soviets and the rule of law. An experiment is to be made whereby the leading party secretaries at the district level up to the highest level of the union are elected simultaneously as chairpersons of the corresponding soviets; if they fail to be elected, they would also be relieved of their party offices. Of course, it remains an open question as to whether this move would signify any real control by citizens over one-party rule. In any case, the autonomy of agencies acting outside the party will need to be guaranteed in a far firmer and more complex manner—a process that can take a long time in the USSR.

In the course of democratic reforms within the Soviet system the party will have to confront other challenges, apart from those already discussed. The existing situation—in which the entire power elite is organized within the party as a social group that is dependent on the party for its livelihood and is subject to quite strict discipline—may well have to be used as an instrument for promoting radical reform. For instance, it would be impossible to abolish, restructure, or reorganize all the enormous management mechanisms in the economy (e.g., to disband the industrial ministries and other administrative departments of economic management in their present form, thus affecting the livelihood of hundreds of thousands of people, and so on) without employing all the "customary" authoritative methods and exerting the absolute power of the party centers and their apparatuses.

The enormous power concentrated in the hands of the party authorities is the only effective force capable of resisting any claims by certain groups of the power elite (e.g., the army, police units, and the centralized office of economic management) to put their own interests first in the course of the reform. Until the basic economic and social processes for advancing perestroika through the system are at least put into motion, and until they, too, begin to align themselves with the reforms, the political leadership cannot renounce the opportunities provided by the type of power that already concentrated within the party.

Institutional Possibilities for the Expression of Different Viewpoints

As already noted in other contexts, the Soviet system originated and developed under conditions in which its survival depended above all on its ability to achieve at any price a few selected and centrally determined goals. This was an advantage during the revolution, the war, and the extensive, noncapitalist industrialization. The Soviet system originated in a country where the social structure and the corresponding structure of interests had for many years been very primitive; there were practically no large social groups involved along democratic lines in political action against absolutism. The tradition of autocratic political decisionmaking, and of absolute power wielded deliberately and arbitrarily by the ruler and his bureaucracy, had been entrenched for centuries.

This tradition underpinned the concentration and centralization of power and political decisionmaking in the Soviet system as it evolved after the October Revolution (in conflict with Lenin's original ideas about revolutionary power—ideas which did not in fact determine reality). Any aims, needs, and interests (as well as the corresponding views) other than those foreseen and programmed from above appeared to obstruct the working of the system. Consequently, the system developed a number of mechanisms that served to suppress anything opposed to its central purpose. In many respects, these mechanisms operate to this day. One of the most important tasks of Gorbachev's reforms is to remove them finally, so that they will cease to influence behavior and thinking.

With the origin and later development of the Stalinist system, a diversity of interests in society naturally appeared to be less important than the unity of social interests and their agreement with the central will as well as with the priorities set by the center of political power. The increasingly simplified and, under Stalin, vulgarized version of Marxist ideology provided justification for these tendencies. The official ideology maintained that the conflicts of views among various social interests and needs actually played a politically important and progressive role in societies where class antagonisms and struggles for influence on political power prevailed. After the victorious socialist revolution, these class struggles continued—and ideology justified the system of mass political and police terror, the curbs on the expression of different interests and views, the censorship, and so on. But the diversity of social interests in the structure of Soviet society was accorded almost no political significance. On the contrary, the main goal for Soviet society was the "moral and political unity of the Soviet people," which, in the ideological view, somehow existed irrespective of the treatment given to various social needs and interests of the different groups constituting the Soviet people.

In line with this, the main task for the political system in the USSR was to ensure that this unity of Soviet society was actually expressed. If unity was to be politically created and expressed—if it was to be achieved democratically on every concrete question—the interests of large and small social groups, of work collectives, and of individuals had to find political expression; then, on this basis, the common united interest had to be sought—but this requirement was ignored by Soviet official ideology for many decades. After 1956 it did seem for a short time that the official ideology would allow the problem of unity and diversity of social interests in Soviet society to be analyzed, and that conclusions could be drawn for the construction of the political system; but following Khrushchev's overthrow such moves were again suppressed.

Political practice was governed until recently by Stalin's theory that Soviet society is made up of just three great social groups—the workers, the kolkhoz farmers, and the intelligentsia. As there is no class antagonism among these groups, according to Stalin, there is no need to worry about how contradictions and differences in social interests should find expression in the political system. The main problem is to ensure the expression of unity. This concept of the Soviet social structure is, of course, quite inadequate as a basis for considering how opportunity for the expression of diverse social interests, needs, and views is to be institutionally guaranteed. More precisely, the concept marks the beginning of a deliberate distortion of the problem. Among other things, it obscures the fact that Soviet society is divided into large groups according to the place occupied by people in the decisionmaking process, in economic management, and in the life of society altogether. It is as if the diversity of interests, the distinction between those who manage and those who "are managed," did not exist— as if that had disappeared together with private ownership, because those who manage enterprises are no longer the private owners.

For decades this subject was under the strictest taboo for Soviet ideology, partly because Trotsky criticized the bureaucracy for being a social stratum over the heads of the working class, and drew radical conclusions from this contention. Only recently has discussion begun about the evident fact that social groups linked with managing different processes in society have their own interests, which they try to promote against the interests and needs of the groups whose work is the object of management.[28]

Indeed, discussion is starting to develop in Soviet social science about the structure of society overall. For instance, Tatyana Zaslavskaya points out that it is not enough to divide society into specific classes, which are special social groups. Included among the largest social groups are not only classes but also nations and nationalities, urban and rural populations, and workers by hand and by brain (i.e., groups traditionally recognized in Soviet ideology as well). But Zaslavskaya goes on to say that "to reconcile the basic interests of these groups . . . is far from adequate for dealing with contemporary problems." Current policies and their corresponding mechanisms need to reconcile and adjust the "interests of groups representing various departments, sectors of the economy, types of enterprise, various regions, community types (e.g., new and old, large and small towns; urban and rural type communities; large and small villages), . . . work groups according to profession, skills and posts held, socio-demographic groups," and so on.

The picture of Soviet society thus becomes incomparably more clear-cut and alive than in the traditional simplified ideological version. And such ideological concepts as "the interests of all the people" appear not as cliches but as aspects of structured, complex social reality. "The general criterion for defining groups," writes Zaslavskaya, "is in the basic differences between certain aspects of their positions in society; character of work, their place in the management of economic or community affairs, level and structure of incomes, residence type, ethnic affiliation, etc. After all, groups of different status usually have different interests, and bringing them into accord mutually and with the interests of society as a whole is, in fact, the aim of politics."[29]

When this is seen to be the aim of politics in Soviet society, it will not be far to the conclusion that the political system must, in that case, enable the most diverse social interests (including those conflicting with each other) to actually find expression and define themselves—if it is to be at all possible "to bring them into accord mutually and with the interests of society as a whole." And if, in practice, changes in the Soviet system are directed toward this end, they will represent one aspect of its democratization. Of course, the system cannot be said to have prevented the differing interests of social groups from finding any expression at all. Certain institutions have existed in the form of "mass organizations," such as trade unions, youth organizations, and sport and other special-interest organizations. The problem, however, is that the system has thus far offered very few opportunities for the direct organization of these interests. Even then, the organizations in question provide no scope in which the various social groups can act independently.

The "mass organizations" in the Stalinist system did not really aim either to give expression to the special interests and needs of their members or to assert these in the political decisionmaking process as means for possible pressure on the authorities. Rather, the opposite was true: The aim was to concentrate the holders of various special interests into the largest possible organizations, where their special needs would be subordinated to the decisions and priorities of the political power centers. Of the two functions that are common to special-interest organization in any political system—that of defending in a politically effective manner the special interests of members, and that of integrating these interests into more general political priorities and decisions—the "mass organizations" of the Soviet system fulfilled only the second.

In the past, these organizations operated chiefly in one direction—from the political power center to the groups organized in the "mass organizations." Their feedback role was quite inadequate. They failed not only to exert sufficiently strong "pressure from below" on the power center but also to ensure a simple flow of effective information to the authorities about the situation, needs, and interests of the groups organized within them.

The "mass organizations" were given this status in the Soviet system quite intentionally, in accordance with Stalin's ideological postulate (a one-sided interpretation of Lenin) about such organizations as "transmission belts" through which the "will of the party" reaches "the masses."[30] The purpose of political power was to subject to its control all social interests, including nonpolitical ones. And the only way to satisfy these interests legally was to belong to one of the "mass organizations," which, as political bodies, could exert political control over nonpolitical activities.

What does this mean in practice? A motorist in the USSR joins an automobile club, as anywhere else in the world; but this special-interest organization is included in the "mass organization" called the Union for Co-operation with the Army, Air Force and Navy. A student who is interested in botany can work in a group (where she will have at her disposal a microscope, literature, and help from adult specialists); but to do so, she has to be a member of the Young Pioneers or the Komsomol, which are explicitly political bodies.

Thus "mass organizations" in the Soviet system ensure that anyone wanting to satisfy his special interests and needs has to do so through joining huge monopoly political organizations that are subordinated to the party apparatus and to the state as well. The main purpose is to politicize any special-interest activity and to prevent any group from organizing independently, decentralizing its management, or self-administering. Almost all "mass organizations imitate the Communist party in their organizational structure and internal set-up: They are centralized; they have district, regional, and nationwide (central) committees; they maintain internal discipline on the basis of "democratic centralism"; and they retain extensive paid apparatuses that control the groups' initiative and self-management in line with the aims of political power.

Through these apparatuses the "mass organizations" also come under the nomenclature procedure; that is, their officials are imposed from outside by party authorities. Naturally, the elections in these organizations are formalities; without the blessing of the party apparatus, the members cannot select their own officials. This is the case with all such organizations, from trade unions to nonpolitical special-interest bodies. Thus far almost all associations and societies have been incorporated into the centralized structures of the "mass organization" monopolies.

Yet some special interests can be accommodated by this type of bureaucratic system. For instance, the trade unions have enormous material and financial resources as well as political power. However, only when the centralized bureaucratic machinery has been set in motion is there an opportunity to satisfy some of the interests of the rank-and-file members. And the decision whether the bureaucratized, centralized "mass organization" will throw its whole weight behind certain interests is made not by the members but by the complicated political machinery of the apparatus, with the decisive voice going to the party.

Certain nonpolitical activities, such as sport, can receive quite considerable support under the Soviet system. But the price is politicization of those activities, using achievements (such as sports victories) as matters of political prestige.

Thus, any reform of the Soviet political system that is to mean genuine democratization must start with special-interest institutions. It is possible to prepare the ground for this democratization (i.e., for autonomous action by interest groups) even within the existing organizations. The main requirements would be as follows:

1. Free the existing "mass organizations" from being ordered about by the paty (and sometimes the state)

apparatus. That is, enable them to exert pressure against the political authorities, as a means of communication "from below" between the authorities and society and not only as "transmission belts" from the centers of power downward to society.

2. Change the policy whereby officials of these organizations are, in effect, imposed (or at least approved) from outside by the party apparatus according to the nomenclature rules.

3. Introduce genuinely democratic relationships between members and the administrations of the special-interest organizations (including real secret elections with several candidates, and so on). And radically reduce the official apparatuses and subordinate them to the membership—not the reverse.

4. Carry out a radical decentralization of authority within the "mass organizations," thus providing scope for self-managing initiative by the members and abolishing the obligatory endorsement of activity "down below" by the headquarters.

5. Allow diversity and autonomy for a variety of interest trends within the "mass organizations." (One can envisage, within the unitary youth organizations, autonomous sections for students and young workers. On the principle of voluntary federalization, such autonomous sections could join in an umbrella political organization such as the Komsomol.)

Granted, the current reform movement in the USSR has not yet produced any clear concept of a program for such changes. But many of these ideas are now being discussed openly in official speeches and documents.[31]

As in the Communist party, numerous changes will probably be made in the various special-interest organizations in the name of new methods and style of work, though not with the aim of making structural changes in the established institutions. However, if such changes tend toward the aims just mentioned, they could be the start of a democratization process that, in the future, could develop into institutional changes capable of preventing a return of the stereotypical "transmission belts."

In the longer term, however, the Soviet political system will be faced with more complex and fundamental questions in connection with institutional guarantees for the expression of varying interests, needs, and views. If democratization is to lead to truly radical reform of the political system, differences of interest, need, and opinion will in time have to be viewed not as instruments for achieving uniform goals preordained by the Party but, on the contrary, as forces that by their very diversity are capable of developing a multiplicity of initiatives, of posing various alternatives, approaches, and means of handling social problems.

As in the economy, so in the political sphere it is possible to manage affairs either by supporting and furthering factors of intensive development (i.e., new methods and types of activity) or by restricting and suppressing them. The institutionalization of interests in enormous monopolies of centralized "mass organizations" has thus far held back the factors of intensive development in the wider (not purely economic) sense. The system is based on the principle of "what is not permitted is prohibited." That is it lays down explicitly which—and in what form—interests can be expressed and find political application. Then all possible interests have to be squeezed into the permitted forms; otherwise, they cannot find legal and politically relevant expression.

A political system designed to support intensive development factors (again, not in the economic sense alone) must rest on the principle of "what is not prohibited is permitted." This principle refers in practice to a legal norm that sets out the means by which special-interest organizations, associations, societies, and so on, can be formed; and then, within this framework, every group or association enjoys its own autonomy. It can set up, disband, or change the organizational forms of institutions for expressing interests, needs, and opinions; and the political authorities (state and party) have no power to limit this autonomy above and beyond what is provided by the law.

For the USSR this is a long-term matter. But even in the present initial phase of the reform, quite a lot has changed relative to long-established practice. Perhaps thousands of associations, clubs, and interest groups have emerged by public initiative. Some are even politically inclined, in the sense of being discussion clubs concerned with the subject of reform (perestroika) policies. The political profiles of some are, to say the least, rather questionable. For instance, the association called Pamyat not only works to protect historical monuments but also is developing a notably archaic and conservative ideology of Great-Russian nationalism, anti-Semitism, and support for Orthodox religion.

It is not yet clear what the future holds for this trend toward association according to the principle of "what is not prohibited is permitted." The fact is, however, that these newly formed organizations are not being forcibly banned, nor are their organizers being charged by the police—and that in itself is a considerable change from the recent past. Of course, these organizations may yet be regulated by a law on association thus far unknown in the legal code of the USSR.[32]

The problem of how and in what manner provision can be made for various sectional and group interests to be expressed and asserted in the decisionmaking process by institutional and politically appropriate means is not confined to those interests that can be articulated in special-interest organizations (i.e., the interests of professional groups, women, and various cultural and sport activities). At least three important areas of special-group interests fall outside these organizational forms, and their institutional position in the political system needs to be established differently. These are the interests of local communities in both rural and urban settlements, the interests of (primarily non-Russian) nationalities, and, finally, the interests of work collectives (irrespective of the type of job) in state enterprises, cooperatives, and various institutions such as health, education, science, and culture.

It is not possible within the scope of this study to make a detailed analysis of the problems connected with the prospects for institutional expression of these specific group interests. The subject is so complex that it would require a separate and extensive analysis for each of the three cases. But very briefly and simply, it can be said that (as in the case of those interests represented by special-interest organizations) the ethnic, community, and workplace interests have thus far been expressed in the Soviet-type political system only through institutional forms that have enabled them to be subordinated to the central will; the bearers of these interests were made the executors of the central political will, instead of being agents capable of autonomous action in the political decisionmaking process, partaking in political decisions, adopting their own standpoints, and defending them in the democratic process of seeking the common interests of society (and the state).

The problem of special ethnic interests is of exceptional importance in the USSR—on the one hand, in view of the multinational nature of the state and, on the other, because the dominant nationality (Russian) has gradually been turned into a minority.[33] Furthermore, it should be remembered that outright suppression of certain nationalities (or nationality groups or minorities in some areas)—which numbered among the typical features of the original Stalinist system—has left very bad memories in the minds of its victims. The declared principles of nationality policy— especially the right, recognized by Lenin, of each nationality to create its own independent state (embodied to this day in the constitution of the USSR as the right for national republics to secede from the Union)—were trampled underfoot for many decades. Under Stalin those who uttered expressions of "bourgeois nationalism" (i.e., views based on the principle of national self-determination) were subject to mass executions and imprisonment—and to this day some of the political prisoners in the USSR are people accused of this "crime." Indeed, tolerance toward expressions of nationalism in the Soviet system is still minimal, whereas the trend toward a multinational state would, of course, demand maximum tolerance.

A satisfactory and more democratic handling of the relations among nationalities is among the most serious challenges for Gorbachev's reform policy; in a sense it is the touchstone for perestroika. A satisfactory result within the framework of the existing constitutional structures might be possible. But it would require that the declared rights of the various state and administrative formations, from national Union Republics to autonomous ethnic regions (especially their autonomy on matters of substantial importance for the given national community) should not remain on paper but be exercised in practice. It would also mean a halt to the policy of gradual denationalization in territories originally occupied by a national majority. This is happening systematically: In conjunction with economic development, mass transfers of labor power belonging to other nationalities (not always Russian) are being organized by the state. In some cases the original nationality constitutes only a minority in its own national republic. As for the towns in non-Russian territories, it is typical that about half or even a majority of the population is made up of other (nonindigenous) nationalities. The associated problems and growing national tensions can be eliminated not through legal or institutional changes but only through changes in the actual policies.[34]

Despite the enormous importance of the question as to whether nationality relations can be progressively democratized, I do not share the view that the accumulated national tensions now rising to the surface in the form of demonstrations and mass protests (in Kazakhstan, Armenia, the Baltic republics, and so on) are of a nature to threaten the actual existence of the USSR. These nationality conflicts are quite varied in nature. Some are regional conflicts rooted in the relations among smaller (non-Russian) nationalities, as in the Caucasus. Others are conflicts provoked by oppressive policies directed against national, cultural, and religious customs (a problem especially in Central Asia, where the issue is linked to contemporary Islam). Still other conflicts are more political in nature—especially when they represent efforts to take the national state out of the Union of Soviet Republics altogether. This is typical of the Baltic republics, which, having been attached to the Soviet Union after World War II, experienced an interwar period as independent national states.

The idea that nationality conflicts of such varied origins could actually emerge as a united and politically coordinated force capable of causing the disintegration of the USSR seems an unrealistic one to me. It is really the reverse of the Stalinist ideology, which perceived nationalistic interests and views as being "anti-state" and thus politically dangerous. Such interests and views had to be suppressed in the interests of maintaining the USSR as a state. Although I do not support the view that nationality conflicts are politically dangerous, I do believe that the Soviet political system cannot be democratized in the absence of a substantial increase in autonomy for the different nationalities. This is a matter not of the right to national folklore but of the right to the political opportunity to formulate the interests of the national community independently and to speak out effectively in their defense when political (and economic) decisions that affect them are being made.

The problem of local community interests, both rural and urban, can be solved in the spirit of democratization only by developing the local (communal) authorities as organs of local self-government that would also perform the key functions of state power and administration in the localities. Such councils (i.e., lower-level soviets) already exist in the Soviet system. However, they grew out of the original self-governing, revolutionary councils ("councils of workers") to become merely the lowest link in the state administrative machinery. Their dual function—as local (communal) self-government bodies but also as organizations through which the state had to carry out its administration—was originally intended to provide a guarantee of democracy (no bureaucracy could be independent of self-government); but under the Stalinist system of local soviets, only the second function actually developed. The soviets turned into the lowest organ of state administration, dependent for everything (from finance and budgeting to staffing according to the nomenclature) on the higher, bureaucratic state authorities. Some of these, up to the Supreme Soviet of the USSR as a special pseudo-parliamentary formation, were also termed "soviets." In place of the principle of "no bureaucracy that is independent of the local self-government" came the principle of "no local self-government that is independent of the bureaucracy."

A move in the direction of democratization would depend on two main changes: First, an economic base would have to be provided to ensure the autonomy of the local self-governing bodies (i.e., the local soviets) in the localities and towns. They would require independent financial resources—that is, resources not tied to "allocations" to the local budget from the higher state authorities. This would involve the gradual establishment of an effective local taxation system and levies on profits from state enterprises and cooperatives working in the area of the given local soviet.

Under the present system, the local soviets are economically and financially dependent on the state enterprises in their areas. From nursery schools to transportation to the maintenance of public roads, community affairs in the smaller towns and localities are in the hands of enterprises working in the area—not under the control of the soviets, because they do not have the money. Great attention is being devoted in the present phase of Gorbachev's reform to making good what has been neglected for decades in this field. There is criticism especially of the "leftover approach," which is taken when enterprises use only surplus resources to meet the social needs of their employees. Moreover, a number of matters are decided by the departmental ministry under which the enterprise falls. As yet, however, no real effort has been undertaken by the reform program to make local self-government bodies (the soviets) economically capable of conducting community policies and being politically responsible for them.

Ideological sophistry surrounding the concept of "self-government" (or "state power") tends to obstruct such a move rather than showing a way out. The official ideology behaves as if the very term *soviet* were a guarantee of the democratic, self-governing character and constitution of the local authorities.

The second main change that must come about by degrees, if a radical reform of the existing system is to be truly successful, is to establish the local soviets as organs of "power and self-government"—especially in the way elections are conducted. There must also be a change in the relationship that will develop within the soviets between the elected officials and the paid apparatus. These questions are repeatedly discussed in official speeches and documents, but they have not been resolved. Only some limited "experiments" with new approaches have been tried.

If the reform is to be taken seriously, the outcome must meet two requirements: The members of local soviets must be elected from several candidates (in secret elections), and the method of nominating candidates must enable locally based special-interest organizations and work collectives to act freely and have the decisive voice in making nominations. Furthermore, the paid staff must be effectively under the control of the elected members of the soviet.

The new Soviet leadership is aware of most of the problems mentioned here. In particular, the decisions taken by the 19th All-Union Conference of the CPSU in June 1988, as well as the measures flowing from those decisions, include definite proposals that should resolve some of the problems. (This subject will be treated more fully in the next section of this chapter.)

Most questions connected with institutional guarantees for the articulation of sectional and group interests, needs, and opinions are not specific to the Soviet system in its endeavor to democratize. Similar problems exist in every democratic political system. So it is possible to extrapolate from the experience of democratic systems in general many measures that should be adopted by the reform in the USSR. This is true for large social groups with various professional interests, for ethnic interests, and for communal self-government in localities and towns.

The problems specific to Soviet society—and, therefore, new both in practice and in theory—concern the role and possible self-management of work collectives in noncapitalist enterprises. Granted, even here some ideas can be gained from history; there is, for instance, the experience of the Yugoslav system of worker self-management. But basically this is a new problem that has never been satisfactorily resolved.

The key difference between the Soviet and the capitalist system is that the whole matter of economic decisionmaking in capitalist society (where the production and consumption of goods and services are concerned) is separate from the system of political democracy. The economy is managed as an independent, autoregulative system according to its own motivations and criteria. In the Soviet system the relations between the economic and political systems will still be different, even if radical systems reform is successful. In a socialized economy the decisionmaking process—that is, management of the economic system has to be incorporated into the democratic decisionmaking system. The key question is now: How is this to be achieved without simultaneously threatening the dynamic of intensive economic growth?

No answer has yet been given to this question, either in theory or in practice. Only attempts have been made at an answer; new solutions are being sought. Although various countries have made experiments in reforming Soviet-type economies, often with rather negative results, there is no unified concept for the new system that is needed.[35]

A problem in this connection is the part that can and should by played by work collectives in linking political democracy with economic management in a noncapitalist economy. Work collectives consist of the people who produce, who perform work in the production process; at the same time they are the people for whom production and work takes place, those whose needs and interests should, after all, play a large part in deciding the priorities in the economy. The Soviet system in its Stalinist guise simply used an ideological phrase: The party and state authorities decided "in the name of the working people"; the work collectives were required to carry out these decisions (the plan) and possibly deliver extra effort, which would lead to overfulfilling the usually quantitative planned targets. This "movement of socialist competition," which grew out of the Stakhanovite movement (named after the miner Aleksei Stakhanov), was, after several decades, converted into an apparent "initiative from below" with bureaucratic records of what was done.

Among the first themes in Gorbachev's reform program was the clear declaration that "the working people" can consider themselves the masters and owners of the means of production only if they genuinely decide what to do with what they own.[36] This idea was soon linked with an organizational structure to express the role of workers in Soviet enterprises as "owner-managers"; these self-governing organs of the work collectives have the right to elect the leading managerial staff in their enterprises, up to the director. The system is gradually being introduced experimentally on an increasing scale.

In reality, however, this is no more than a beginning in a new approach to tackling the problem of how to link democracy with the economic management process. Elections of directors are not in themselves the solution. Everything depends on the degree of autonomy in the economic position of an enterprise where the workforce is about to establish its self-governing bodies and further what is (or will be) the link connecting these self-governing bodies with the whole political-power system and with administrative bodies apart from and above the enterprise level.

It is not within the scope of this work to deal thoroughly with the substance of the basic questions arising in this connection. Nor can they be precisely formulated. But the following brief remarks on the subject are called for in relation to our present theme. It is not possible within the existing institutional system to give expression to the interests, needs, and views of the work collectives, which in the Soviet (noncapitalist) social structure are among the key social agencies. An entire system of new bodies is required, consisting of organs of self-governing producers. In the widest sense, these encompass people working in nonproducer activities such as services, from health to science and culture. One could speak, for example, about organs of enterprise self-government or workplace self-government; the actual label is not important.

Of crucial importance, however, is the status they will have after the Soviet enterprises that are to set up self-governing bodies have undergone reform. Insofar as these enterprises do not have adequate scope for independent action—including deciding about prices, products, long-term investments, workforces, the procedures involved not only in marketing their products but also on the capital market, foreign trade relations, and so on—their self-governing bodies will also lack sufficient opportunity to exert any substantial influence on the production process and on matters of management.

Another important issue concerns the means by which the self-governing bodies are to be formed. Included in this process are such details as the method for nominating candidates for elections; accountability to the electorate; the actual composition of the bodies (in terms of the proportion of workers and technicians); the managers' participation and influence; and the possible influence of agencies outside the enterprise that are important for its operation and prosperity (e.g., customers, suppliers, and creditors). Also included is the procedure by which their competence will be legally defined and guaranteed—that is, regarding which matters they can decide outright, where they have only advisory powers and where they have the right to veto, and what their relations will be with other organizations in the same workplace, especially the trade unions. The fundamental requirement if enterprise self-government is to be successful is, of course, that officials cannot be imposed from outside by the party apparatus or state authorities.

The third key problem relates to the linkage between the self-governing work collectives and the system of democratic (elected) organs of state administration—that is, the soviets in the case of the USSR. The only satisfactory solution would be a linkage ensuring both sufficient political influence for the enterprise self-government in the process of decisionmaking and sufficient scope in which noneconomic interests and needs can influence decisions on economic policies, including planned development programs and priorities. If enterprise self-government results simply in the opportunity to promote the sectional, short-term interests of a given producer group, and does not ensure coordination from the standpoint of overall social needs and interests, it will surely be defeated once more by the bureaucratic principle under the pretense of expressing the "interests of the whole." The critical factor in this connection is open, long-term discussion on these matters in the USSR, drawing on the experiences in Yugoslavia, for example. Unfortunately, such discussion is not yet under way.[37]

The purpose of my brief reflections about the prospects for institutional expression of diverse interests in the USSR is not to solve the concrete problems involved. My purpose is to indicate that development in the direction of institutional guarantees for expressing diverse interests is possible by means of progressive reforms even within the existing political system in the USSR. This process could start as soon as certain radical steps have been taken. Above all, it will be necessary to do away with the situation whereby the centers of absolute power connected with the party apparatus have total control over all movement in society, including the power to set up several new institutions (e.g., the self-governing work collectives). In any case, a period not just of years but of decades will be required before a new, democratic institutional system of guarantees can be established in which diverse social interests, needs, and views can be voiced in a politically relevant manner during the decisionmaking process.

It would be a mistake to suppose that the problems connected with the character, functioning, and development of these institutional forms are merely of secondary organizational concern. This is not an organizational problem but, rather, a social process, the intrinsic aim of which (to create a collective will among certain elements in society, and then in society as a whole) is unattainable without institutional structures. For the will of collectives cannot develop and take shape except on an institutional basis. The collective will is created by a different process, the main requirement for which is "to establish the kind of institutions where the creation of the collective will and its functioning appear, in a sense, to be similar to that in biologically given organisms."[38] Failing that, society cannot, in part or as a whole, "think" and "wish."

In this sense, then, the process cf providing institutional guarantees for expressing social interests, needs, and views is closely linked with the essential innovation of ideology. The Stalinist institutional system promoted the existence and dissemination of a vulgarized official ideology. Democratization of the institutional system would be bound to encourage innovation and to make possible a pluralism of views. It could never produce an ideology as sterile and deadening as Stalin's. Of course, an impulse in the direction of democratization will also be needed from the sphere of political and civil rights and freedoms, with which we shall be dealing shortly.

The Law-Based State in the Soviet System

A few years ago, the official ideology of "true socialism" would have maintained that a demand for the "socialist state" to turn into one based on the rule of law meant transplanting "bourgeois ideas" into Soviet conditions. For the reform program today, however, "creating a state governed by the rule of law is a matter of fundamental significance."[39]

Granted, such a state is identical neither to political democracy nor to the Western-type pluralistic parliamentary system. It does, however, offer a highly important and realistic means of eliminating the system of unrestrained political dictatorship, with its absolute power and total control over all society. Similar processes have taken place in the West, too, where the transition from absolutism to constitutional monarchy can be regarded as the first stage in the evolution of the constitutional state. At first, the autocratic system of political power was retained, but rules and limits were set that the otherwise autocratic ruler and his bureaucratic apparatus had to observe. Hence the way was opened for asking the question, Who is the source of the decisive (i.e., legislative) power that lays down the rules and limits that are binding on everyone? And it was possible to answer this question, in the republican-democratic spirit, to the effect that the source of power lies in "the people." That answer, in turn, opened the way to the Western-type democratic political systems of modern times.

It would be pointless, of course, to compare the problems now being addressed in the USSR with the situation during the historical transition from absolutism to constitutional monarchy in the West. But I have mentioned this historical aspect to avoid automatically equating the demand for a state based on the rule of law with the type of relationships between state and society (i.e., the citizens) existing today in, for instance, West European countries, which describe themselves as being governed by the rule of law but are, in addition, pluralistic parliamentary systems. This coexistence is not necessarily the case during all stages in the evolution of the law-based state. It was not the case historically in the West, and it cannot automatically be assumed for the Soviet system today. Under certain conditions it is possible, and developments may move in that direction (but not necessarily always) even in Soviet-type system. In particular, certain historical factors in the Central European countries of the Soviet bloc have strengthened the tendencies toward such coexistence (e.g., Czechoslovakia in 1968), and it has been historically confirmed by the efforts to change the system in Poland and Hungary.

Why is the demand for a state governed by the rule of law to be seen as a matter of fundamental importance for the development of the political system in the USSR? To answer this question, we have to realize that an intrinsic feature of the present Soviet system is the existence of a dual structure of political power. On the one hand, there is the officially proclaimed power structure, declared by the Constitution and numerous laws, which is made up of elected representative bodies (i.e., soviets at various levels as organs of power and administration). The relationships between this structure and the society is also formally regulated by laws and other legal measures.

Alongside this political power structure, on the other hand, is another that is not regulated by the Constitution or by statute. Its relationship to society and its competence are not clearly defined by any published legal code, but these factors are nevertheless supreme from the standpoint of real power and its execution. This second decisive power structure is composed of organs of absolute power based in the Communist party (representing a merging of the party and state apparatuses)—organs that have already been discussed in connection with the so-called leading role of the party. It still includes an extensive managerial network within the command system for the economy, as well as police and armed forces that are not subordinated to the soviets (indeed, they are commanded from the center of absolute party and state power).

The demand for a law-based state in the USSR signifies, in effect, an endeavor to escape from this situation. It is a demand for abolishing the "shadow power structure" that has hitherto been subject to no law and is in reality the supreme power structure. In that sense the demand for this type of state is of truly revolutionary significance given the reality of the Soviet political system; it represents a striving for a qualitative change in the system. For insofar as it has been possible to speak with truth about a system of total control by political power over society (and over individual citizens), then this was possible thanks to that "shadow structure" which created absolute power and was not subject to any control by the society it ruled.

Of course, one cannot expect that, as the reform program progresses, the move toward a state based on the rule of law will abolish at a stroke all the actual relationships and behavioral patterns stemming from the "shadow structure." Yet it can—if carried out with determination—lead to ever-stronger curbs on this power structure—curbs that will increasingly subject it to the law and hence reduce its ability to exert total control while not being under any other control itself. And where authoritative elements persist in the system, they may be subjected to the law, at least to the extent that there is some democratic control over the way the authoritative instruments of power are wielded.

Here, too, the demand for the law-based state can play a very significant role in providing new and practical ways for delimiting the so-called leading role of the Communist party. For the time being, a certain scope for the party organizations to intervene in decisionmaking by the state authorities will undoubtedly be retained—in the interests of the reform program itself—because situations will arise requiring an integrating power and opportunities for authoritative intervention. Reform of the political system cannot, in the initial stages, rely on democratic mechanisms because they simply do not exist. While they are being established, it will occasionally be necessary (as frequently noted in this volume) to use authoritative methods of government, including authoritative interventions by the Communist party.

All the more important, then, that these interventions by the party do not reinforce the existing "shadow power structure" (with the party apparatuses as its core); but the party organizations should also be subject to the law in the process of making and executing power-based decisions. In other words, the first step in eliminating the existing structure of absolute power in the Soviet situation is to subject it to the law and the legal code, regulating and restricting it wherever it cannot be abolished at a stroke.

If this to be accomplished, however, extensive reform of the law will be necessary. The provisions of a whole body of legislation (substantially affecting even the Constitution) will have to be revised. Thus the demand for the law-based state cannot be met simply by calls for observance of the law; it will have to mean revision and new legislation in whole areas of the legal code (i.e., regulation of the relations between authority and society, and between social groups and citizens).

So, if the state in the Soviet system is really to develop according to the rule of law, a very complicated and difficult process will ensue. The life of society will be profoundly affected as new relationships are established between the power holders and society, between the managers and the objects of management, and between the state (the social collective) and the citizen (the individual).

To understand at least the basic problems involved, we must analyze the subject from two angles. First, we must examine the development of the structure of political power and administration—as well as that of the law and its enforcement—by looking at the whole system for managing society. Then we have to examine the position, interests, and behavior of the social agencies, groups, and individuals being governed and managed. This second angle necessarily concerns a whole range of problems connected with civil rights and political freedom in a Soviet state system governed by the rule of law.

With regard to the political system, establishing a state based on the rule of law in the USSR poses a problem that is also familiar in the Western world. Briefly, this problem is related to the so-called division of power, which concerns the relationship between the legislative and the executive—that is, the relationship between the elected representative bodies (composed of deputies) and the administrative machine (composed of professional officials, who are bureaucrats in the narrow sense of the word).

How to ensure that those who make the laws really have the decisive influence in making political decisions and in carrying them out? How to ensure that these elected bodies are not, in reality, subordinated to the bureaucracy, which, on the contrary, is supposed to be subordinated to and controlled by them? So long as the question of the division of power is not satisfactorily resolved, the rule of law cannot function: The exercise of power would not be subject to the law, and those who execute the law would not be subordinated to the legislators.

This problem is typical of any state based on the rule of law, irrespective of its economic, social (class), and political nature. But in the USSR, the problem is all the more complicated by the "shadow structure of absolute power" and the existence of ideological mystification. Soviet ideology has traditionally refused to recognize that the "Soviet-type state" could have such problems: Lenin put it all quite differently. Indeed, his concept of the state deviated significantly from that of the so-called law-based state. He assumed that the soviets, as state organs, would simultaneously act as organs of "self-government by the people" and could, therefore, combine the legislative and executive functions. In the spirit of Marxist reflections about the Paris Commune, Lenin had in mind a situation whereby state coercion and state power would reside not in a separate apparatus but directly in the "mass organizations" of the people (the proletariat).

According to Lenin's concept, which was embodied in the 1918 Constitution of the Russian Socialist Federal Republic, the soviets were to ensure that a society organized as a Soviet state would govern itself in much the same way as would a mass public organization. The basic organizational cells were to be soviets in villages, towns, and cities. Under the 1918 Constitution, elections to these soviets were to be held every three months. In small communities, where technically possible, matters of public administration were also to be decided by meetings of all citizens.

All the higher organs of state power and administration were elected at congresses by delegates from local soviets. These congresses were to be held at the lower administrative levels (in the small districts known as *uyezdy*) once a month, in larger districts once in three months, and in regions at least twice a year. The All-Russian Congress of Soviets was also to be held at least twice a year.

The congresses of soviets elected their executive committees as the supreme authorities in their territories. These committees gave account of their work at each congress. Thus the top authorities in the districts and regions, as well as at the center, changed at least twice a year. The Council of People's Commissars (the government) was directly accountable to the Central Executive Committee (the state-wide authority), which was to be changed twice a year as well. This committee could suspend or cancel any decision, and politically important measures had to be presented to the government for examination and approval.[40]

What, then, was the nature of this Soviet state with respect to the construction of the organs of state power and administration? If all the aforementioned measures had been carried out, it would really have been a "semi-state"—that is, an organization based on constantly newly elected (rotating) representatives of the people in the localities and towns, who temporarily (during congresses) served as direct representatives of the higher state power and controlled the executive. Not even the top executive bodies were independent of this control for more than six months—until the next congress of soviets. With justification, Lenin could have described such a system of state power and administration as a form in which self-government merged with the state.

In reality, however, this system was never put into operation—not even during Lenin's lifetime. Important sectors were always operating on the basis of other principles. In these sectors, power was in effect removed from competence of the soviets and entrusted to various specially empowered bodies. This applied both to the economy (during and after the years of "war communism") and to military and security matters. The actual decisions were prepared and ultimately issued by a select body of professional revolutionary cadres; they were then implemented by various authorized agencies, which were, again, under the control of this select body.

Lenin was aware of this situation, and he spoke about it openly. He explained it as being due to exceptional circumstances (revolution and civil war), as well as to the backwardness of Russia, the lack of education among the masses, their inexperience in public affairs, and so on. He stated candidly that, owing to historical circumstances, the soviets, instead of being the means whereby the people governed directly, had become bodies that ruled for the people and in their interest. And he admitted that the goal of an immediate identity between "the masses" and the organs of power had not been reached. In the last years of his life, Lenin thus directed his attention to the means by which the already existing Soviet bureaucracy could be placed under effective control by the masses. The system of worker-peasant inspection seemed to him to provide the key element, since the soviets alone could not play the self-governing role expected of them.[41]

After Lenin's death, the Soviet state developed along lines quite different from those he had had in mind when he formulated his concept of the "semi-state"—that is, the merging of state and self-government and the dying away of the state. By degrees, all the key areas of life—from the planned economy to cultural and political matters to the armed forces and the police—came to the governed by centralized bureaucratic apparatuses that, in reality, were not subordinated to the soviets; indeed, they had originated, operated, and established themselves independently. Apart from the soviets, there also arose a whole system of control and administration by the Communist party and its apparatuses, to which the soviets were then subordinated.

Moreover, a radical change took place in the organization and structure of the soviets. At first in an informal manner, then (from 1936 on) under the terms of the Constitution, they ceased to be bodies of the "Paris Commune type" and assumed a parliamentary representative form. Currently, all soviets, from the lowest to the highest, consist of fixed-term deputies whose mandates are guaranteed for two and a half years in the lowest soviets and for five years in the highest soviets. The institution of congresses of soviets has disappeared. The higher organs of power are not constituted by the lower, as in Lenin's day; they are elected directed by the population, as in parliamentary republics.

As distinct from "bourgeois parliamentarianism," however, "Soviet parliamentarianism" has retained the principle that the voter does not have a choice among candidates from different political organizations (i.e., parties). The permanent deputies in the Soviet system run unopposed in their constituencies. Formally they are nominated by "workers and their collectives" at voters' meetings, but in fact they are chosen and presented to the electorate by the party apparatus. In the system envisaged by Lenin, rotation was a permanent feature: Elections to local soviets four times a year, and congresses of soviets several times a year, guaranteed that control could be exercised from below over the organs of power and administration, even without the medium of political parties. How criticism and opposition views were to be voiced was not a serious or separate problem in this administration model. It was dealt with (though only in theory) through the principle of rotation for officials and by the congresses of soviets, to which the delegates depended for reelection on the support they received from the voters. Similarly, the problem of bureaucracy in the state administration did not exist (again, at least not in theory). Executive power, too, could always be taken over by new people—that is, by nonprofessional deputies to the soviets who sat on the Executive Committee. In theory, the paid professional bureaucrat could not get into key positions, certainly not for any length of time.

Since most of what Lenin envisaged was never implemented in practice, and since the measures that had been taken were gradually abolished, we cannot continue to pay lip-service to the word *soviet* and fail to see that a relationship between power and society completely different from Lenin's theoretical concept about a "state of soviets" has developed in the USSR. We must remember that Lenin spoke of a "higher type of democracy" than parliamentary democracy.

Now, under the label of *soviets* are bodies that, in practice, are parliamentary in type (in villages and towns they are bodies of local representation) as far as the relationship to society is concerned: Permanent deputies (often professional politicians from various political institutions), elected at fairly long intervals, meet to take decisions (laws). The executive administration is entrusted to professional bureaucratic offices that are supposed to be controlled by the elected bodies but, in reality, run their departments independently.

By proclaiming the demand for a state based on the rule of law, Gorbachev's reform program has clearly come out in favor of a realistic course. It recognizes reality and intends to change it by means that are reasonable, not ideologically utopian. Its aim is not a return to Lenin's concept of the "commune-type" state, for that has been proven by history to be an impracticable way to manage a modern industrial society. The division of labor (which affects the management of both industrial and nonindustrial work in society) and the need for specialized and professionally qualified managements are problems that have proven to be far more complex than was envisaged by socialist thinkers, including

Marx, in the last century. These problems bring to mind the conflict between earlier ideas and present reality in the context of commodities, the market, and money in non-capitalist socialist societies.

Thus the development of the state based on the rule of law merges in the USSR today with the development of "socialist parliamentarianism"—not with the "transcendence" of parliamentary-type bodies. Consequently, political reform under the slogan "strengthening the role of the soviets" has a different meaning than the slogan "all power to the soviets" of 1917 and shortly afterward. Today the main challenges are as follows.

1. The Soviet system must ensure that political decisionmaking takes place in the soviets and in the bodies (e.g., commissions) under their control, and that decisions (including bills) will not be delivered to them from outside (i.e., from the centers of absolute power within the existing, but not legal, "shadow power structure"). In other words, reform process must ensure that what are designated by law as organs of power should really be organs of power and not mere instruments of nonconstitutional power centers.

2. The Soviet system must ensure that the deputies to the soviets are really elected and not merely "approved by the electorate," as was the practice when voters were able to vote for a single candidate, or to not vote at all. Of course, in this case several candidates will be needed for each constituency. And the system for nominating candidates will have to be changed. Thus far, in theory, the principle of "unlimited opportunity" for making nominations has been in effect, but that will remain just a declaration so long as the law has not clearly established who has the right to nominate candidates, and by whom and in what manner the final decision will be taken as to which candidates will actually be included on the ballot.

Where there is only one political party, the procedure must be quite precisely defined in law. The organizations or groups of citizens that have the right to nominate candidates must also be clearly defined, and an explicit provision must be made regarding the right to exclude provisionally nominated candidates from the final round. Certainly a democratic procedure cannot rely on the current system, in which "everyone" seemingly has the right to nominate "anyone" at voters' meetings; but in which the real selection procedure for the final round takes place under cover in the political (party) offices without any clearly defined competence or opportunity for control from outside.

3. The Soviet system must ensure that, in soviets at all levels, the executive is subordinated to the deputies and effectively controlled by them. In this respect the present reform is justifiably taking a course opposite to that originally envisaged by Lenin. This course aims to separate the position of deputy from that of the executive staff, such that the paid staff will be barred from becoming deputies to the soviets. (In that case, they would be controlling themselves.)[42]

Gorbachev's reform program has adopted an unusual way to deal with the relationship between the soviets and the corresponding party committees in their territories. In increasing the authority of the soviets, the principle to be applied is that their chairpersons will, as a rule, be the leading party secretaries of the corresponding town, district, regional, or republic committee of the CPSU. This step has been presented as a democratic one, for the party secretary will have to be elected by all citizens in the soviet elections. If this does not happen, however, the party post would be "re-examined."[43]

Although this argument is plausible (depending, of course, on how democratic the election system for the soviets turns out to be), it is not altogether convincing. Combining the chief state and party functions in the hands of one person at all levels of the hierarchy (from towns and districts to the highest authorities in the USSR) embodies a principle that tends to run counter to the customs of a modern state based on the rule of law. It is a characteristic of this state that no part of the power structure (and no individual) should have a power so concentrated that effective control could not be exerted over its use. Misjudgments or possible mistakes at one level should always be correctable by another independent link in the political system.[44] It is doubtful whether, given the existing situation in the USSR, with its tradition of absolute power and a single political party, this effective control over political power can be ensured by the proposed arrangement.

I am inclined to believe that this arrangement (i.e., the concentration of party and state functions in the hands of one person) has to be assessed in the general context of the reform process. It would imply that the authoritarian principle is retained but that the concentrated power should henceforth be subjected to a certain measure of control. It should no longer operate through the "shadow power structure" (based in the party apparatuses) but be public, regulated by legal norms, and based in the official organs of power, the soviets. An arrangement retaining an authoritative element by concentrating power in single hands can mark real progress on the road to democratization. That, however, would require that a system of public control over the work of the soviets really evolves, that a democratic electoral system is established, and that those who hold power work under conditions of glasnost, with civil rights and freedoms guaranteed. The "shadow power structure" would thus be replaced by a single, public structure regulated by the Constitution and the law, which, under Soviet conditions, is a step forward.

The same is true of the supreme organs of state power. Whereas the members of the Supreme Soviet were once elected directly by the voters, the new supreme body is to be constructed in a more complex way. It will be called the Congress of People's Deputies, and its members will be elected not only on a territorial basis (as representatives of the lower-level soviets) but also as delegates from various political organizations (the party, trade unions, youth organizations, etc.) and cooperative, cultural, and scientific bodies. The congress will elect the Supreme Soviet and also its chairman who, according to the principles mentioned above, will be the general secretary of the Party Central Committee. But the congress, itself will be the supreme organ of state power, meeting once a year to deal with fundamental constitutional, political, and socioeconomic matters.[45]

Although in formal terms this concept is reminiscent of Lenin's idea that the supreme organ of state power is a "Congress of Soviets," it does not really represent a return to his vision of a system of soviets. It adopts a few elements from his idea, but it lacks the entire institutional base with its system of congresses of soviets from bottom to top and its constant rotation of officials. The present reform project substitutes for "rotation of cadres" the principle that no one may occupy a given post for more than two consecutive terms. As the term of office is set at five years for soviets at all levels, rotation occurs every ten years; Lenin's idea, by contrast, was to rotate twice a year.

From these aspects of the current project for reforming the power structure in the USSR, it follows that the evolution to a state based on the rule of law will be unique. The main features of this evolution are determined by history, by the present situation, and by the actual prospects of the evolution of political power in the USSR for the foreseeable future. These reform concepts cannot be proclaimed as a "generally binding" model for the "socialist state based on the rule of law." Insofar as one can speak about the organization of political power as being "socialist" or "bourgeois," both forms are always, and in every country, subject to specific historical conditions and other influences. Just as the law-based state in France differs from that in West Germany, it can be (indeed, must be) different in the USSR as well as in Czechoslovakia or Poland. Any other approach would risk repeating the old habit of proclaiming the forms for organizing society in the USSR as being the embodiment not of historical conditions but of so-called universal laws of socialism.

The main problem in establishing a state governed by the rule of law is the need to remove the dual power structure—that is, the official constitutional structure and the "shadow" existing outside the law and linked to the merging of party and state. Thus far, the new reform policies have dealt with this problem quite inadequately. The law-based state is incompatible with political-police supervision over society—as it has traditionally prevailed in the Soviet system.

In short, just as the real political and legislative decisions regarding laws were made outside the soviets, so the real decisions about citizens' rights, about their promotion or discrimination at work, about their prospects materially and in other respects (e.g., foreign travel), and, in general, about what is and what is not permitted or prohibited, are made outside the officially appointed authorities. Very often they are made behind the scenes in the party and security apparatus, according to information and reports about people's political behavior (a function of "reliability"). Such information is gathered in many ways, at workplaces and in places of residence, with the help of officials from various political organizations and of secret agents from the political police. The information, withheld from the persons concerned, is often used to decide their careers and even their personal lives.

Although the complicated system of political-police supervision that collects such information is not mentioned in the Constitution or in other legal provisions, every citizen knows about it only too well based on personal experience. Two agencies can use the services of this mechanism: the political police (KGB) and certain sections of the party apparatus.

The entire judicial system (encompassing the courts as well as prosecutors, judges, and defense lawyers) is dependent on these mechanisms. Until recently certain "nomenclature cadres" enjoyed virtual immunity from the law; proceedings could be brought against them only with the agreement of the appropriate party apparatus. Moreover, judges often received verbal instructions from party and KGB officials as to how cases should be handled.

In other words, there has been—and to some extent still is—a vast apparatus of political police supervision within the Soviet system that lies outside any effective control by the public. Its authority is not defined in any published legal provisions, and citizens have no means for appealing against its actions.

Gorbachev's reform program has thus far touched on this problem very cautiously and only in relation to certain matters. First, the courts have been declared to be independent of the party and other apparatuses, and outside intervention in the work of the judiciary has been publicly criticized. This criticism (e.g., from the press) has revealed the magnitude of such interference, with respect to the liberties that were once taken by uncontrolled officials. It is difficult to believe that the situation is quite different at present.

The dismantling of the political-police mechanism can be accomplished only through new legislation on civil rights and freedoms, after glasnost has strengthened the critical atmosphere, the reform has yielded real successes, and the basic democratic course is felt to be irreversible. Granted, there is already talk about the need to subject foreign policy as well as management of the arms industry and the armed forces to control by elected bodies; but no demand for putting the activities of the political police under such control has been heard thus far, even in a general way. Yet so long as the mechanism for police supervision is not abolished, progress in basing the state on the rule of law will be impossible.

If the Soviet state is to advance along these lines, a substantial change in the legal system is essential. The All-Union Conference of the CPSU held in June 1988 passed a special resolution on legal reform, naming it one of the main tasks in shaping the political system. However, even this resolution states that the approach to legal reform is not yet sufficiently clear. Indeed, the changes required in the legal order have not been formulated with the necessary clarity.

The resolution focuses on the organizational and technical aspects of legal reform—bringing "order" and hierarchy into the law-making process, reducing the number of normative regulations, especially at the level of various departmental orders and instructions, and so on. Attention is given mainly to economic and administrative law, then to criminal law and the courts, and, finally, in rather general terms, to certain changes in the Constitution (with respect to the powers of national state formations, the decentralization of powers in general, and so forth). Education of the public in matters of law is also stated as a political requirement.[46]

The hierarchy of legal norms is a particularly important problem in existing Soviet law. Legal practice does not observe the principle that a higher legal norm is binding on the content of all below it—for instance, on government orders, various operational regulations, instructions from ministries and other offices, and normative acts issued by lower-level (republican, regional, and local) soviets and their offices. In reality, the true meaning of legislation is often lost or completely changed in the dense network of operational regulations issued by the ministries and other departments. Yet these lower-level standards, regulations, and instructions are what really matter, because the everyday work of the whole vast administrative apparatus is guided by them, not by the general letter of the law. The real legislators in the USSR are still, in effect, the ministries and the diverse administrative departments; and the government, not the elected bodies, is at the center. So the executive is placed above the legislature in the sense that the legal measures of the executive decide what is and what is not "socialist legality." According to recent party resolutions, the legal reform will alter this situation and ensure that the law and the legislature are supreme.

If the legal reform fails, the current economic reform will also be gravely threatened. For instance, the new Law on the State Enterprise is intended to give enterprises greater independence and to restrict command methods of planning, thus creating a basis for economic reform. But this measure has been by-passed and blocked by hundreds of normative acts issued by ministries and various administrative departments—acts ostensibly intended to implement the measure but actually weakening it and changing its meaning.[47]

However, these and similar problems can be tackled only if the aims of the legal reform are not confined to certain organizational and technical matters; rather, they must take into account the concept of the law as well as its role and function in society. The party resolution refers to this question in general terms when it calls for consistent application of the principle, "what is not forbidden by law is permissible." Traditionally, the opposite has applied in the Soviet system: "Everything is forbidden that is not permitted by authority."

A fuller analysis of the Soviet concept of law (i.e., of official Soviet legal theory) is not possible here. Let it be noted, however, that the theoretical concept still largely in force to this day is that dating from Stalin's days. It was formulated and forcibly imposed by Andrey Vyshinsky who, while serving as chief prosecutor in the political trials of the 1930s, also occupied the position of head legal theoretician in the Stalin era.[48] This concept sees the law as being essentially no more than a special form, subject to certain regulations, of the orders and commands whereby the regime (the state as the form and "the ruling class" as the socialist content) imposes its will on society; that is, the law manages society's life in diverse areas, from the economy to private personal relationships (in the family, for example). It is primarily an instrument for governing. People in groups and as individuals are the prime object of this government; the legal system turns to them as recipients who have to carry out orders and conduct themselves accordingly. Only in the framework of this basic purpose does the law sometimes "allot" to them the role of participants, protecting their special and individual interests—as in civil law, the work process, and so on.

At best this concept views the citizen as an object of social care. That is, the rights of Soviet citizens are generally understood as their claim on the state, which in turn should use its power and organization to satisfy or protect their basic interests and needs, especially in the social sphere. This approach still underlies the formulations in the USSR Constitution dating from 1977 about the rights of Soviet citizens. All the relevant articles (numbers 40–46) are couched in the same stereotype: "Citizens of the USSR have the right to (work, rest, health care, material provision in old age and sickness, to housing, education and the use of cultural facilities). . . . This right is ensured by . . . (state policy which ensures the growth of the production forces, development of recreational and health provision, various forms of social insurance, housing construction, development of education and cultural facilities available to all)."

Regarding the rights of Soviet citizens with respect to political freedom, a different stereotype applies. Rights such as freedom of the press, speech, and assembly (Article 50 of the Constitution) are guaranteed only insofar as they are "in accordance with the interests of the socialist social order and are directed to strengthening it." The freedom to do scientific research and artistic work (Article 47) as well as the right to set up organizations (Article 51) are guaranteed by the Constitution only "in accordance with the aims of the building of communism." True, the current reform policy of glasnost has introduced some substantial changes, but the present Constitution still contains nothing but the above formulations about political freedoms. The question as to who decides what is "in the interest of socialism" or "the building of communism" remains unclear from the standpoint of constitutional law, but in practice it has traditionally been a matter for the party or the police.

If the Soviet state is to evolve as a state based on the rule of law in the tradition of European civilization and political culture—and it appears that this is what Gorbachev has in mind—the legal reform will have to be directed to gradually transforming the way in which the role and significance of the law have hitherto been understood. It will have to address all the practical problems that this situation poses for the legal system, including legal regulation of the relations between the state and the people, both collectively and as individual citizens.

But the traditions of European civilization and political culture require that the law be seen primarily (though not solely) as the right, secured by state power, of people (citizens, collectives, and groups) to that measure of autonomy vis-à-vis other social agencies—especially the regime, as in that case they will be able to manage for themselves (i.e., decide independently on their actions and choose among alternatives the behavior that seems best from their own point of view). Autonomy and independent decisions must be the rule; exceptions can be made only by the law. The principle "whatever is not forbidden by law, is permitted" has to be understood in this sense.

A number of consequences follow from this principle, both for social agencies (e.g., for the right to association and assembly insofar as it applies to whole social groups, and also for the independence of enterprises and their workforces) and for individual citizens. For instance, the political rights of citizens cannot be restricted by political dictums such as "accordance with the interests of communism," but only by definite legal provisions (e.g., under criminal law, which declares certain behaviors or views, such as the propagation of race hatred, to be indictable).

Problems of this nature have, as we know, been sensitive political and propagandistic subjects in connection with the persecution of defenders of human rights in the USSR. Such persecution has continued to be the case long after Stalin's day, especially in the 1970s. The fact that valid legal standards are not always observed and citizens are denied some of the rights and political freedoms embodied in the legal code is not peculiar to the Soviet system. We see not only in other dictatorial regimes but, in a different guise and along different dimensions, in Western democracies as well.

This matter has assumed special significance in the Soviet system for three reasons. (1) Three decades ago, the Soviet system was exposed by Khrushchev as a system marked by the discrepancy between what was proclaimed and what actually happened in terms of mass political terror and crimes perpetrated by the state. Inevitably, the years of Stalinist terror, masked by the slogan about "a higher type of democracy" than the formal political equality of citizens before the law in the West, have had lasting consequences. (2) Long after these crimes were revealed (up to 1986), the authorities behaved in a manner that aroused distrust. (3) Soviet citizens have often been demonstratively denied rights that, from the standpoint of the traditions of Western civilization and political culture (especially democratic, including socialist, traditions), are an indispensable elementary guarantee for the democratic way of life—namely, the right to think and act in accordance with one's convictions, even when that is disagreeable for the authorities and does not correspond with their demands.

Gorbachev's reform program of 1986–1988 has certainly changed things for the better in many respects. The atmosphere of political police supervision has been lifted, and the practice of glasnost has embarked on a course that should logically lead to a new concept of civil rights and political freedoms essentially compatible with European political culture and legal traditions. Even then, Soviet conditions will necessitate a long-term process in which to overcome the historical legacy in this respect.

Briefly, the view of the citizen as an object of state providence, together with the emphasis on social rights (especially for whole groups of the "working classes") and the counterposing of these economic and social rights to political rights and freedoms (especially for individual citizens), stem from two main historical sources: the history of Russia, and the criticism by Marx and Lenin of "merely formal equality" for people under capitalism.

The Soviet legal order began to evolve after 1917 on the basis of economic, social, and cultural backwardness in Russia. The masses were illiterate and lived under semifeudal conditions that combined serfdom with pre-capitalist collectivism (as in the Russian *obshtina*, meaning village or commune). The citizen—created in the West as a political reality by the bourgeois revolutions in the United States, England, and France, and already formed by the Renaissance and the Protestant Reformation—did not exist in Russia as an active political factor. Russian society had not participated in the development of ideas from the Renaissance to the Enlightenment. The influences of these ideas reached only a narrow social stratum of intellectuals, some of whom opposed the 1917 revolution and were considered "counter-revolutionary."

Official Soviet ideology, primarily as expounded by Lenin himself, based the concept of law on the nineteenth-century Marxist critique of bourgeois society. A polemic with the concept of "the natural rights of men" advanced by the Enlightenment philosophers also served as a starting point for reflections about law and its social role. Marxism emphasized that, in capitalist society, the human being is divided between an abstract, formally free citizen equal to all others, and a socially determined being who is subjected to class inequality and oppression even in a system of "civil rights and freedoms."

In this connection, Marxism also stressed that the actors in history are socially defined people, primarily large groups and classes. Consequently, for Marxism the most important actors in history appear to be collective in nature, as reflected in the Marxist ideological vision of the future under socialism and communism. The problem of the individual's legal status in a future socialist society is not considered. One reason for this is that the ideology had originally been dominated, first, by the utopian idea that human relations based on commodity production, money, and material inequality would rapidly disappear; and, second, by the expectation that the state would soon wither away, political-power relations would vanish, and self-government by "voluntary associations of producers" would take their place.

These ideological notions about overcoming "merely formal equality" were transferred after 1917 to a society that had not yet experienced the formal equality criticized by Marx—an environment in which Western-type civil society was unknown. Consequently, although these notions formed the official "ruling" ideology, they could not in fact determine the shape of things in a political and legal system that had to be capable of establishing itself in Russian reality and of saving the country from the catastrophe of social and economic collapse facing it after the Revolution. The actual problems, needs, and traditions in the Russia of those days gave rise to a political system and legal order that, while adopting many ideological slogans from the Marxist vocabulary, created relations between the regime and the people that enabled the former to impose its will (i.e., its "plans" for the economic and social order) at any price. Thus an autocratic totalitarian system evolved, exacerbated by the specific characteristics of Stalin's personal dictatorship. The concept of law and its role in society matched this reality, although it relied for its ideological justification on the Marxist critique about "merely formal equality" for citizens under capitalism and about stressing social and collective rights as opposed to "bourgeois individualism."

Of course, compared with this historical background, the current reform program—with its demand for a state based on the rule of law and the accompanying legal reforms—is an enormous advance. Fortunately the party resolutions themselves see further development as a long-term process, the present steps being just "the beginning of the great task" of legal reform to be implemented "in the next few years."[49] Indeed, the establishment of a new concept of law in society as a real factor in social development depends on the progress being made in establishing the new economic, social, and political conditions corresponding to a modern industrial-type civil society. In particular, the importance of the individual citizen in the legal order can be truly effective only to the extent that changes are made in the status and degree of autonomy enjoyed by the individual in the economic, social, and political spheres.

A structure of economic relations based on private ownership of the means of production is not essential here. But what must be put into effect if the individual's role in economic and social relations is to be increased is the principle that his status depends directly on performance (especially in terms of initiative, creativity, and so on). If the principles of a performance-based society do not become a real part of life in Soviet society, one cannot expect any substantial change in the role of law—especially in relation to the rights and freedoms enjoyed by citizens as individuals. But the process involved will be a very lengthy one, depending on the successes and failures of the economic reform program and the new social policy in the USSR.

With regard, as well, to the political rights and freedoms of the individual citizen, real changes are conceivable only within the framework of the given institutional system, not in opposition to the system. One cannot expect political rights to begin with the freedom of people to join together in organizations capable of competing in elections with the monopoly position of the Communist party.

However, the reform will probably give rise to a gradual increase in the role and importance of every individual within the system of permitted collective institutions—from work collectives to special-interest organizations and to the Communist party itself. At the same time, the opportunities for individuals to voice their opinions publicly will continue to expand—given glasnost, in the sense of freedom of expression, criticism, and plurality of views.

Citizens who have gained greater autonomy in this context cannot be reduced again to passive objects for manipulation by political power. In time, they are bound to demand more, not less, autonomy. Undoubtedly this emancipation of the individual will be a long-term process, full of contradictions and obstacles, but nevertheless offering hopeful prospects.

In examining the law-based state from this standpoint, we find that the cardinal factor in advancing it is the new status for citizens as people to whom the law guarantees the necessary degree of autonomy. The chief guarantee of success on the road to such a state is not merely legal reform along the lines being applied in the reform program but also (indeed, primarily) the process known as glasnost. The 19th Conference of the CPSU adopted a separate resolution on glasnost that is seen as offering a real opportunity for all citizens and social agencies to obtain information (except for that which is explicitly designated by law as state secrets), and as providing the right and real opportunity for citizens and agencies to express their opinions, criticisms, and attitudes on various alternatives in the political decisionmaking process.

Seen in this way, glasnost can be identified with the political and legal conditions that, in the European political culture, signify freedom of expression and opinion—and thus, in effect, freedom of the press. Of course, the history of Soviet society and the Soviet political system is still unique in certain respects—for instance, the fact that the media are controlled either by the state or by official organizations. Yet the boundaries of glasnost, which initially served merely as an instrument to facilitate public criticism—

an essential element in any reform process—have been visibly extended. Now it is opening the way to confrontation among various (often officially undesirable) views and attitudes. It has led to a situation described in the current Soviet terminology as a "pluralism of opinions" and also as "freedom of conscience." (A special law regarding freedom of conscience is being prepared that should include not only religious freedom but also the freedom to express unofficial, non-Marxist views, the freedom of artistic creation, and so on.) This law will go far beyond the limits of the provisions contained in the 1977 Constitution.

Only in the context of all these processes will Soviet society see the gradual emergence of citizens as autonomous individuals in their relationship with the regime. Such a social phenomenon was, of course, unknown under the traditional Stalinist system. And only when these autonomous individuals have lived for some time as a social fact will it be possible for a meaningful analysis (not just an ideological controversy) to be made of the similarities and differences between West European and Soviet developments in the areas of human and civil rights and political freedoms.

3 / International Aspects of the Soviet Reform Program

Perhaps even more striking than the changes that have taken place in domestic politics since Mikhail Gorbachev took over have been those both in Soviet foreign policy and in the attitude of the official ideology toward problems in the world today, the role of the USSR in the world, and a number of important international issues. When the present minister of foreign affairs declares in a keynote speech that "the fight between two opposing systems is no longer the decisive tendency in the present epoch,"[50] what has emerged is not only a new ideology but also a new basis for the overall concept of international relations—one that is strongly influencing Soviet policies.

From roughly 1985 to 1986, the responses from Western politicians, journalists, and many "Sovietologists" tended at first to be dominated by a skeptical attitude toward the new vocabulary of Soviet foreign policy. It was widely believed that the changes in this area were primarily a product of the state of emergency in which Gorbachev found himself with his program of "accelerated development." He needed economic aid from the West and reductions in the burden of arms expenditure—hence the attractive verbal offers in the sphere of foreign policy. The initial Western skepticism was prompted both by the long experience of the Brezhnev era and by the fact that the changes in Soviet foreign policy, which initially appeared to be sweeping proposals, were not fully worked out and had not been preceded by international negotiation. For instance, in his speech of 15 January 1986, Gorbachev proposed to eliminate all nuclear weapons by the year 2000; and at the 27th CPSU Congress in February 1986, he proposed a new "arrangement of the world." In addition, a major political aim pursued by Soviet policy was to prevent further development of the SDI program and to halt altogether the armaments policy that the Reagan administration was supporting and implementing.

However, subsequent events in 1987–1988 made it obvious that such an approach to the new Soviet policy was one-sided and that it seriously underestimated the importance of the changes in the USSR. On the one hand, the new ideology continued to develop. Under the "new political thinking," people started asking important questions concerning international relations in the world today, in terms quite different from those heard in the past. On the other hand, certain practical steps were taken indicating that the Soviet leadership was very serious about its new course in foreign policy. The agreements on destroying intermediate-range nuclear missiles and on withdrawing Soviet troops from Afghanistan were examples of such practical measures. As a result, a more constructive approach began to prevail in the West. The new features of Soviet foreign policy are no longer regarded mainly as propaganda designed to gain time and gather forces for a new offensive to achieve the old goals of superpower, hegemonic policy. On the contrary, they are seen as the possible beginning of a new course that is setting new goals and employing new means.

In short, a more optimistic tendency is beginning to prevail. The demilitarization of East-West relations is regarded as offering real hope, and the traditional conflict between East and West is seen as a phase that, in time, may be succeeded by relations of a predominantly cooperative rather than confrontational nature.

As soon as this optimistic attitude becomes too pro-
nounced, however, its supporters will have to ask, Is a far-
reaching transformation of Soviet foreign policy really possible, given that the USSR is one of two superpowers in
the world today, mainly (but not exclusively) thanks to its
military strength and not to its economic potential and
political influence? Does the USSR not need military means
to hold the Soviet bloc together? Is not optimism about
the role that the USSR can play in the world a case of
the wish being father to the thought? And, of course, an
even more skeptical question—maybe with a pessimistic
answer to match—is still being put by those who, despite
developments in the past two years, have maintained a
basic distrust in any changes in communist ideology and
policies.

At present, clearly, there can be no straightforward,
objective answer to these questions. Nor is it possible in
the scope of this work to make a comprehensive analysis
of all the circumstances that would have to be taken into
consideration. Nevertheless, I shall attempt (as before, in
the context of domestic political reforms in the USSR) to
summarize what new departures have been proclaimed
and partly implemented in the field of foreign policy. I
shall also try to point to the prospects that can be regarded
as realistic alternatives. Toward these ends, I shall concentrate on a possible new concept as to how East-West
relations may develop, and on relations within the Soviet
bloc.

Soviet "New Political Thinking" and Its Significance for East-West Relations

The phrase *new political thinking* is officially applied in the
USSR today to an integrated set of ideological concepts

about the modern world—primarily, to the role of the USSR, the relations between capitalism and socialism, and the impossibility of war as an instrument for resolving conflicts in today's world. Although this ideology is undoubtedly linked with the ideological innovations being carried out on the domestic front (in connection with the economic and political reforms discussed above), it would be simplistic to regard the new way in which Soviet ideology views the world as being merely an attempt to project the domestic program into foreign affairs and to use foreign policies to bolster its internal reforms. Granted, this attempt is among the aims of the "new political thinking," and Gorbachev occasionally speaks about it openly. However, after reading his speeches and those by other members of the Soviet leadership, as well as the entire output on international questions from research institutes and by journalists in the press,[51] one is bound to conclude that the roots of the new ideological concepts are more complex and do not stem solely from domestic sources.

In this connection, I think that what we are witnessing is a belated response by the USSR to developments in the world over recent decades. These developments include the crisis in the hegemonic arrangement of "spheres of influence" between the two superpowers, the rapid progress of the advanced industrial nations (and the "scientific and technological revolution") in contrast to the crisis in the Soviet-type systems, and the development of relations between North and South. In short, the USSR is responding to certain events in the past few decades that the official ideology under Brezhnev simply ignored or reacted to quite mistakenly. At the same time, a response is being heard from a new generation in the Soviet power elite for whom the critical experience in the world arena is not world war but the simultaneous existence of different economic and political systems. For this elite, the USSR is indisputably a world power of global importance, ready to intervene in handling problems anywhere in the world.

In a sense, Soviet ideology is only just now coming to grips with problems that the other superpower of our times, the United States, had to face during the first half of the 1970s. It was clear for U.S. politics during the Nixon, Ford, and Carter administrations that changes were taking place in relation to the "bipolar division" of the world and also to the formerly undisputed hegemony of the United States. In the 1970s it was already an accepted fact that, due to the advance of the EEC countries, Japan, and certain other nations, the leading position of the United States on world markets was no longer unchallenged. Only through "tri-lateral" cooperation, taking into account the interests of other countries (e.g., OPEC members) could world economic problems be dealt with.

In the political sphere, particularly after the defeat in Vietnam, it became obvious that not all world affairs were dominated by the stereotype of the bipolar East-West conflict. Processes of "diffusion of power" were taking place within the international community, and "third forces" were grow-ing. Thus it became increasingly evident that many issues, including U.S. superpower interests, could not be resolved by military force. At the level of the arms race between the United States and the USSR, so-called parity was reached in strategic nuclear missiles and the race came to be regulated by agreements (i.e., the SALT agreements of the 1970s) between the two superpowers.

In this connection, efforts were made during the 1970s to subject the prevailing concepts in U.S. foreign policy to critical evaluation. The main objective of the United States was to react constructively to the emerging complexities of problems in the international community. The traditional policy of the 1950s and 1960s, when foreign relations were seen as bipolar and as colored by the military (due to the political and ideological concepts born of the East-West conflict) was gradually replaced by a policy of interdependence that would give due regard to all the diverse interconnections and the mass of contradictions in the relationships of the modern world.[52] This change of emphasis also enabled U.S. foreign policy, and made it easier for the West as a whole, to accept the idea of detente.

On the Soviet side at that time, however—at the height of Brezhnev's fame and power—the ability to respond to the new situation was lacking. At the level of Soviet official ideology, no words were spared in the realm of propaganda about peace; but the main "guarantee of peace" was presented as being the USSR's military strength, which would "deter" all enemies of peace. The United States' endeavor not to allow itself, after Vietnam experience, to be drawn into military adventures in the Third World was exploited by Soviet policy to establish military bases and make armed interventions in Africa. Then, in 1979, the USSR began its military intervention in Afghanistan.

The Soviet leadership regarded the recognition of strategic military parity with the United States as their greatest success, but it also served to reinforce their bipolar view of the world. Instead of seeing this situation as offering an opportunity for changing the policy they had been pursuing thus far, or for adopting a new foreign policy, they attempted to gain the upper hand by devious means: deploying the SS-20 intermediate-range nuclear missiles, building up a navy capable of intervening in any country in the world, and maintaining superiority in conventional weapons in Central Europe.

Some attempts at a different course and new foreign policy initiatives went no further than steps in connection with the preparation and proceedings of the Conference on Security and Cooperation in Europe held in Helsinki in 1975. Although the occasion offered an opportunity for

Soviet policy to move from the bipolar model (with reliance on military strength) to radically new concepts (security based on recognition of mutual advantage, interests, and agreements—on a multilateral basis), Soviet policy continued, even after Helsinki, along the same old lines. The USSR gave most weight to points in the Helsinki accords that corresponded to the traditional interests of Soviet policy.[53]

Only in connection with preparations for the 19th All-Union Conference of the CPSU in summer 1988 did the Gorbachev leadership criticize the policy of those days for failing to recognize the need for a new course, "letting itself be drawn into" the old ways of the arms race, overestimating the potential of military strength, and "underestimating the value of political means."[54]

That was very mild criticism. In reality, Brezhnev's foreign policy became one of the major factors in blocking a new phase in international relations. For many years it prevented new development in international politics for which the United States and other Western countries would have been ready. It was not inevitable that the attempts at a "policy of interdependence" should come to nothing, or that a new version of the cold war should start in the early 1980s during the first period of the Reagan administration. What made the cold war possible, among other things, was the Soviet view that the U.S. variant of the "policy of interdependence" was a sign of superpower weakness that could be exploited for its own superpower ends.

Indeed, Gorbachev experienced a similar unresponsiveness on the other side himself when his attempts at a new course in international relations met with a rebuff during the first phase of the Reagan administration. For a time it even seemed that the situation of the 1970s was being repeated—but with the tables turned, such that the new Soviet initiative would not be received by the U.S. (Western) side as a serious proposition because it was seen (not by the Soviet leadership but by the American president) as superpower weakness to be exploited to one's own advantage. However, this pessimistic alternative did not materialize. In fact, there is reason for hope that this time the inevitability of radical change in international relations would be understood by both competing superpowers— that is, on both sides of the East-West divide.

Yet even if this understanding comes about, it will be merely the start of a lengthy, contradictory, and open-ended process. The outcome will depend on all the participants in the complex international scene. Moreover, that outcome may be not what the participants really want but a combination of their conflicting purposes and practical steps that no one envisaged.[55] That, of course, is the general rule in international relations. Still, it is realistic to hope for some real change for the better.

The Soviet new political thinking is, in by view, also the fruit of a determined effort by representatives of those seeking reform in the USSR to find their own creative answers to the fundamental problems in the world today. To the extent that the thinking of these reformers is shaped by the ideology of Marxism-Leninism (often to a very great extent, as in the case of Gorbachev), it results from a resolute attempt to interpret some of the basic postulates in a humanistic spirit. (The same has been true of domestic policy.) That is one reason why the West should not underestimate the ideological component in the foreign policy course of the USSR. Soviet politicians see this component as a very strong argument in favor of their new line. It helps to implement the new foreign policy even though this policy clashes at times with pragmatic power interests.

From this standpoint the Soviet reform program has acquired a certain messianic flavor; it really represents a kind of "fundamentalism" among modern political trends. This is neither welcome nor even at times comprehensible to those in the West who take a rational and analytical approach to foreign affairs. But it has to be taken into account as an established fact, even though it conflicts somewhat with certain clichés of Western analysts. In the wake of the Stalin and Brezhnev periods, the first having been dominated by the cynicism of power and the second, by the cynicism of corrupt and morally degenerate ruling circles, it is essential for the success of the reform program that Soviet society should experience some renewal of faith in the values proclaimed by the official ideology and official policies. This applies not only to domestic affairs but also, especially, to international policies, through which the traditional Russian-Soviet need to play a messianic role vis-à-vis other nations plays itself out. It is fortunate for the rest of the world when this need is met largely in the spirit of a humanist interpretation of Soviet ideology—that is, in the spirit of a new political thinking that, while frequently self-important, is not aggressive in content. In that case it is possible to tolerate even the quite unpleasant manner in which Soviet propagandists abroad (many of whom were defending Brezhnevism not so long ago) present the new thinking as something that no one in the whole world could ever have thought of before it was proclaimed by the Central Committee of the CPSU.[56]

Let some attempt, then, to describe the main contents of this new political thinking on which Soviet foreign policy is trying to base itself. Very briefly, and thus in a simplified manner, these contents are as follows.

1. The basic and most decisive question, which occupies a key place historically and logically in the whole course of the new ideological concept, concerns the possibility or impossibility of war as a means of resolving conflicts between different systems in the world today. Throughout

the post-Stalin period, Soviet ideology concluded that while war, especially nuclear war, is totally undesirable, in the last analysis it is a possible and conceivable means for resolving conflicts between the two main systems in the contemporary world (between "true socialism" and "imperialism," between East and West, and between the Soviet and Western-type systems). The official Soviet ideology, in the form it assumed under Khrushchev in the CPSU program of 1961, even maintained that the Soviet system could win a nuclear war.

From this flowed the whole ideological argument in favor of the nuclear arms race. True, Soviet ideology (like that of the West) saw nuclear weapons as "political" weapons above all—that is, as a means to deter a potential enemy. However, should that enemy take the fateful step beyond this barrier of deterrence, then Soviet ideology regarded nuclear war as possible and the USSR as the probable victor. The possibility of conventional war was regarded in the traditional way as a means for resolving conflicts between states; only if such a conventional war should threaten to turn into a nuclear conflict would a new situation arise.

The official Soviet ideology accepted the notion that peace could be ensured by atomic deterrence (the famous "balance of fear")—a notion shared by the ruling circles in the West. But Gorbachev subjected all these ideological postulates to radical revision as soon as he came to occupy a top political position. The new Soviet ideology now rejects the very possibility of nuclear war, for it would be a "global war in which there would be neither winners nor losers, but in which all civilization could be destroyed."[57] Following the catastrophe at the Chernobyl nuclear power station, it has also concluded that, with the existence of nuclear reactors, conventional war could threaten civilization and all life on earth to an equal degree. For instance, if a power station were to be hit by artillery, a far greater catastrophe than that at Chernobyl might ensue. From this follows the radical conclusion that in the atomic age, with the use of nuclear energy even for peaceful purposes, an unprecedented situation has arisen in which an armed conflict represents the threat of catastrophe for humanity and all life on earth.

In that case, it is necessary to declare that war has ceased to be a possible instrument for resolving conflicts between the different systems in the world and must be excluded from the means employed in international politics. As this situation is fundamentally different from that of Lenin's time, his statements about the inevitability of war are now obsolete.[58]

This conclusion about the impossibility of nuclear war (and of conventional war as well, given the existence of the nuclear industry) leads logically to the rejection of deterrence by means of nuclear weapons. "The balance of fear" is now declared to be a factor that cannot permanently ensure peace. Although parity between the USSR and the United States in nuclear weapons and missiles continues to be proclaimed as "an historic success for socialism," these weapons cannot be regarded as a guarantee of peace. So long as peace relies on fear, the situation is not only one of equal security but, under certain circumstances, also one of "equal insecurity"—that is, equal danger for both sides. According to Gorbachev, "Continuing the race in nuclear arms necessarily increases this equal danger and can reach the point where even parity ceases to be a factor for military and political restraint."[59] Indeed, the arms race has its own dynamic that, despite parity, can escape the control of both participants.

The "new political thinking" has drawn a number of related conclusions. First, it is necessary to reevaluate the existing concept of security among nations (i.e., "the centuries-old manner of thinking and acting" based on the logic of the *pax romana*, which derives from the one-sided view that one's own security is guaranteed by possessing the greatest possible military strength). Military doctrine must also be reevaluated. Thus the concept of "mutual security" (which is guaranteed on the basis of respect for a diversity of interests) and a defensive military doctrine are concrete products of the "new thinking." Of course, at present both are merely stated concepts (and may therefore be regarded skeptically as propaganda); for in reality the "balance of fear" continues, and Warsaw Pact troops are armed and deployed in a manner that is far from conforming to a purely defensive military doctrine. But it cannot be denied that the ideas generated by this new thinking are producing propositions of a more concrete nature. The demilitarization of East-West relations is conceivable in the light of these ideas, although it will be a long-term and contradictory but nevertheless decisive process.

2. In line with this basic premise, the new ideology also draws new conclusions with regard to the relations between "capitalism and socialism" on a world scale. While in the nuclear age an antagonistic relation still exists between these two socioeconomic formations, it can proceed "exclusively in the form of peaceful competition."[60]

In the past, peaceful coexistence between the two social systems was defined by Soviet ideology as "a specific form of class struggle between them"—a struggle in which ultimately "the socialist world system" must be the outright winner.[61] The new ideology sees this coexistence as a situation in which "states with differing social orders" live together for an unlimited period of time, but the final goal is not defined as victory for either one of them. It is an open-ended situation. Peaceful coexistence "is not just a condition without war" but "an international order in which cooperation, not military force would prevail," and the resources already expended on armaments serve "to solve the global problems of humanity by the collective efforts of all states."[62]

The most radical statement made thus far in this connection was that made by Foreign Minister Shevardnadze in a speech to members of the Soviet diplomatic service. He explained the significance of the 19th All-Union Conference of the CPSU for Soviet foreign policy. He emphasized that the "new political thinking" rejects the view of peaceful coexistence between different systems as being a special form of class struggle. "Coexistence that relies on such principles as non-aggression, respect for sovereignty and national independence, non-interference in internal affairs and so on cannot be identified with class struggle. The conflict between two opposing systems is no longer the decisive tendency in the present age."[63]

This statement, of course, represented an explicit revision of a fundamental "article of faith" for Soviet ideology. It was precisely this conflict between two opposing systems that was seen as the hallmark for the whole historical era up to the "final victory of communism." So it is no wonder that opinion is divided around such a sharp formulation, even within the new CPSU leadership. Indeed, a few days after Shevardnadze's speech, Politburo member and Central Committee Secretary Yegor Ligachev asserted that "we base ourselves on the class character of international relations. To put the question otherwise causes confusion in the minds of the Soviet people and of our friends abroad."[64]

Despite this clear ideological objection, however, we can assume that the underlying trend both in ideological thinking and in the conduct of Soviet foreign policy is now, and in the future will be, determined by Shevardnadze's type of thinking and not Ligachev's—however devious and intrinsically contradictory the verbal exercises about the "class approach" may be.

The new Soviet ideology has repeatedly stressed that the modern world constitutes "a contradictory unity," that unity exists despite class antagonisms. Consequently, "the common interests of all humanity" have come to the fore. Officially, Lenin is quoted as a thinker who spoke about the priority of interests common to all humanity over class interests and antagonisms.[65] In the nuclear age, with the threat of catastrophe and the extinction of life on earth, this is doubly true. As Pravda declared, "All countries in the world are connected and are dependent on each other, all people live on the same planet; . . . today universal human values have to be given precedence, because the world belongs to people, to the present and future generations."[66] In place of the "conflict between opposing systems," Shevardnadze has pointed to a different key problem: "At the present stage what is assuming crucial importance is the ability to increase the supply of material goods more rapidly on the basis of scientific advance and the latest technology and to distribute them fairly, to renew and protect by joint endeavour the resources essential for human survival."[67]

The new Soviet ideology includes among the global problems of common concern to both East and West not only disarmament but also ecological matters and the further development of Third World countries. Thus the "new political thinking" has ceased to view the Third World countries as merely a special dimension of the conflict between "capitalism and socialism." It is beginning to recognize them as a separate problem in the economic as well as political and cultural senses. In time, we may see a critical reassessment of Soviet policies in a number of Third World countries, especially those in which military bases were established in the 1970s in order to back up Soviet political influence—in the event of a possible conflict with "imperialist interests."[68]

This policy revision, already under way given the new Soviet attitude toward the zones of conflict in Afghanistan, Cambodia, and Angola—would also be a logical outcome of an idea that, according to Shevardnadze, was formulated in 1986 by Gorbachev—the idea that it is senseless to behave as if the USSR were as strong as any possible coalition of opposing states.[69] It was the thinking along these lines that led not only to the excessive arms build-up but also to the establishment and maintenance of military bases by the USSR in distant areas of the Third World— in countries where Soviet interests cannot really be threatened so long as these interests are not perceived as being concerned with an (unrealistic) "world hegemony."

In accordance with this ideologically new concept of peaceful coexistence among different systems in the modern world, the opportunity for discussing the nature of contemporary capitalism and formulating new opinions and ideas was officially given the go-ahead in the USSR. Gorbachev himself outlined the main problems arising in the field of foreign policy.[70] He did so not to give answers but to pose open questions to which the answers had to be sought—because now the "one and only correct Leninist answer" no longer exists. These questions are as follows:

- Is capitalism capable of acting in the international arena not solely in its own interests but in the general interests of humanity?
- Is capitalism capable of renouncing militarization and of operating economically without militarism?
- Is capitalism able to survive economically without neo-colonialism?

Without giving answers to these questions, Gorbachev has pointed to certain facts that could indicate positive answers—for instance, "the rapid development of contemporary capitalism in some countries [Japan, West Germany, Italy] with minimal military expenditure." He has concluded in general that, irrespective of ideological considerations, the USSR "will have to build a safer world together with the capitalist countries."

3. Another essential feature of the "new political thinking" is the emphasis on the complexity of international relations, in regard to multilateral regional relations, relations between certain regional areas, and the interrelations and mutual influence among the military, political, economic, and cultural spheres.

From the standpoint of regional division, Soviet ideology is beginning to move away from the bipolar view of the contemporary world. It is inclining toward both a multilateral understanding of international relations and a polycentric model that allows for the existence of several (rather than just two) power centers. The United States, Western Europe, and Japan are explicitly denoted as "imperialistic centers," and within "the world socialist system" China is expressly recognized as an independent power, separate from the USSR.

The new Soviet ideology regards the problems in four regional centers—the European, Asian, Pacific, and American areas—as being relatively independent. At the same time, of course, the USSR and the United States have interests in several regional centers that fall within their own territories. The idea is that it would be best for each of these main regional areas to work out an overall view of relations that would ensure collective security and cooperation among the countries concerned, roughly on the model of the Helsinki Accords for Europe. As in Europe, the system of regional agreements should provide not only for guarantees of security to the participating countries but also for their cooperation on economic, political, cultural, and humanitarian matters. Although the point is not to do away with the existing divisions into groups and blocs, there would be no reliance on such divisions. In a sense, they would be superseded: The system would be of a "supra-bloc" nature. The Soviet leadership recognizes that this system raises many new and contentious questions that still require elaboration and discussion (on the part of the USSR itself), but he is convinced that such a development offers the only optimal solution.

At the same time, it has been possible to see a positive tendency in the fact that Soviet foreign policy does not tie the settlement of certain regional conflicts (as in Afghanistan, Cambodia, and Angola) to any overall regional "rules of conduct." On the contrary, the accepted view is that the ending of the conflicts is the precondition for any future development.

In terms of the complexity of interrelations among the military, political, economic, and cultural spheres, the "new thinking" stresses the need for a systematic effort to overcome the "enemy image" created over decades in the minds of people on both sides by the atmosphere of competition between the systems. Where stalemates have occurred (e.g., regarding the subject of civil and political rights in the Soviet bloc), the new thinking has opened the door to possible discussion at least a little. True, the Soviet side has officially and unequivocally proclaimed that this is a result of the reform policy's respect for the "ideals and principles of socialism." It has also rejected the idea that there could be any "giving way to pressure" from abroad. But that makes little difference to the actual outcome.

In the speech already quoted, Shevardnadze emphasized that "the image of the Soviet state" is "an important aspect of its existence in the international community, in the civilized world today." The main concern here is to overcome the legacy of the past in the sense of "excluding any possibility of conflict between our behavior and our ideals."[71] Translated from diplomatic formulas into normal language, the fact to be recognized is that the USSR has been its own worst enemy. Indeed, it continues to be so wherever and whenever, under the cover of phrases about socialism and democracy, it acts as a dictatorial totalitarian state and behaves in international relations as a superpower out to maintain its hegemony by any means, including force and suppression of those weaker than it.

The new concern with the Soviet image abroad would be unthinkable outside the context of the reform process. It is a genuinely new element in Soviet official conduct in the international forum, although it is still confined largely to declarations of intent.

In the same category of genuinely new elements is the demand formulated by Shevardnadze (or, more precisely, his account of the demands made by the Party Conference in relation to the mechanism of foreign policy) that a definite "constitutional mechanism for adopting foreign policy decisions" should be established. Such a mechanism would ensure effective democratic control over the decisionmaking process in the field of foreign affairs. Shevardnadze explicitly emphasized that this measure had been "earned by the people through their suffering." That is a veiled way of saying that crucial decisions (including those such as the pact with Hitler in 1939 and decisions on military actions, in consequence of which large numbers of Soviet troops may have fallen, were in fact arrived at by a handful of the most powerful people (members of the Politburo) apart from any constitutional bodies and procedures. The same reasoning leads to the demand for "a legislative procedure that will ensure control over all departments concerned with activity in the field of the armed forces and the armaments industry"; only the competent elected organs of state will be able in the future either to decide on "the use of military forces outside the state borders" or to determine the means that are to be devoted to defense. In the future, the military budget is not to be secret.

These are all principles that, if implemented, would undoubtedly improve the "image of the USSR" and allow the Soviet Union to be received with greater confidence "in the civilized world of today." Another politically important element in the "new thinking" concerns the means whereby recognition is given to full sovereignty and the right to a "special road" for all members of the Soviet bloc. The USSR has renounced the practice by which it assumed the right to decide what is and what is not "socialist," and to use force against those who strayed from these ways.

As in the domestic field, the reform program has not yet created a new economic, social, or even political reality. The new thinking has neither fundamentally nor irreversibly changed the reality of East-West relations, those between the USSR and the Third World countries, or Sino-Soviet relations. What has changed is the political atmosphere of the international arena, insofar as the Soviet program and political attitudes play a decisive part in that respect. This atmosphere is certainly one aspect of the international situation, and the change must therefore be seen as something new in international relations. But it is only one element of many, and it is far from being the most important for the reality of world politics as a whole.

Most important of all, perhaps, is the fact that the long stagnation of numerous pressing international problems has at last been ended; things are moving again, and various alternatives for resolving questions in dispute are opening up. Moreover, the prevailing trend is not confrontation and conflict but, rather, the opening up of opportunities for cooperation. In short, the changes in the Soviet ideological concept known as the "new political thinking" are creating space for and reinforcing the positions of all (politically diverse) forces in the world today—forces that in the past have striven for cooperative, not confrontational, solutions to international conflicts but have found no possibility of gaining support or practical help from Soviet foreign policy.

It would appear that the new thinking in the USSR is really providing the opportunity for the United States to renew its attempts, interrupted in the 1970s, aimed at developing its foreign policy along the lines of the "politics of inter-dependence." Despite all the caution and mistrust felt in relation to the ideological-propagandistic aspects of the new Soviet program, various quarters with influence on U.S. foreign policy will probably agree in the future that here, too, it is necessary to adapt to the new trends. Symptomatic in this respect was the fundamental examination of U.S. foreign policy "after Reagan" written in 1988 by two former secretaries of state (from different parties), Henry Kissinger and Cyrus Vance.[72] The authors state that by the end of the century a marked change will have occurred in some of the pillars on which the global world order was based after World War II. The United States, meanwhile, has long since ceased to hold the atomic monopoly, and its share in the world economy will not, by that time, have reached even one-half of what it was forty years ago. Not only Japan and the EEC countries, but also a number of developing countries will continue to figure as independent economic powers. Although, according to the authors, the East-West conflict will continue to present the "old security problems," it will be accompanied by numerous other points of conflict including "state supported terrorism and the international drug trade."

In other words, the basic approach to the world situation already known in the 1970s as the "politics of inter-dependence" is now returning in another guise. Assuming that the USSR will actually apply its "new political thinking," this approach could yield results quite different from those in the Brezhnev era. Kissinger and Vance also noted that for many allies of the United States, the threat from the reform leadership in the USSR appears to have lessened, and that from this standpoint the West's dependence on the United States has been reduced. This, they say, will require that the United States work out a more subtle and complex form of political leadership. All in all, of course, it could create a more favorable situation for tackling the United States' economic problems, specifically through reduced expenditure on armaments.

Both Kissinger and Vance give an explicit warning against the fact that U.S. policies toward the USSR are based on suppositions about the intentions of one Soviet general secretary. After all, no one knows yet how successful he will be on the home front, and a successor could ultimately pursue a different policy. Moreover, the policies of perestroika and glasnost, however attractive to the West, are internal affairs of the USSR on which the West has very little influence.

Kissinger and Vance agree that some aspects of the new thinking are unrealistic propaganda that fail to offer the prospect of radical change in the reality of East-West relations. This is especially true of Gorbachev's ideas about total nuclear disarmament. They regard as utopian, for instance, the vision of a non-nuclear Europe, and they consider that the principle of effective deterrence (including nuclear deterrence) of a potential enemy remains unalterable in relation to an opponent who possesses conventional superiority in important areas and, in addition, possesses nuclear weapons that can reach the whole of Europe from its own territory. (It is well known, too, that neither the French nor the British government is in the least sympathetic to the idea of giving up its own nuclear potential, regarding it instead as a necessary guarantee for the "policy of deterrence," which in their view has ensured forty years of peace in Europe.)

Nevertheless, both Kissinger and Vance recommend that it is high time for NATO to redefine its aims. Following the U.S. presidential elections, it is necessary to embark on extensive work that will result in a new concept for NATO's tasks and plans in the coming decades. Within a year there should be a revised structure for the organization and its armed forces, as well as clear guidelines for the next round of negotiations with the Soviet Union on arms control.

If the Soviet reform program continues to progress successfully, U.S.-Soviet relations will likely move in these directions. Over the years, this could lead to a truly new quality in the relations between East and West. But the process involved will be a lengthy and difficult one.

This conclusion applies also to a relatively independent area in East-West relations—that is, to Soviet policy in Europe and to West European policy toward the Soviet bloc. This matter will be discussed in greater detail in the following part of this chapter. At this point, however, let it simply be noted that the new watchwords of Soviet policy, especially those concerning Europe as a "common home," really amount to no more than the emergence of a new political atmosphere.

All the definite steps taken thus far, such as the U.S.-Soviet treaty on the removal of intermediate-range missiles (the INF treaty) and the withdrawal of Soviet troops from Afghanistan, signify a new quality in the conduct of the USSR. For the first time, we have witnessed the destruction of a whole category of weapons, and not merely an agreement banning an increase in their production. For the first time, too, the USSR is withdrawing from a militarily occupied territory without any guarantee that the regime the military intervention was designed to support will ultimately survive. Here we have something more than propaganda. Yet the steps taken have been insufficient to bring about a change in the quality of international relations, particularly Soviet relations with countries not counted among its "allies."

Although there is still hope for possible changes not only in the attitudes of the U.S. and Western governments but also in those of China and the Third World countries, there is extreme caution, too, born of long experience with the conflict between Soviet propaganda and reality. For instance, the official Chinese press assessed the situation in August 1988 as follows: "Gorbachev's 'new thinking' has aroused universal interest. Now people are worried whether the Soviet leadership can transform this 'new thinking' into concrete deeds and really resolve certain open problems together with the countries concerned. Deeds, not words, decide."[73]

Certainly, as with all great visions of a "world order," there will be big differences between what the Soviet new thinking originally proclaimed and what results in practice. There is no purpose in discussing such differences in any detail before they actually occur; nor does their inevitable existence detract from the value of the Soviet initiative in pointing to the possibilities of a "new world order." That initiative opens the door to a new and unprecedented development—namely, the move from conflict to cooperation.

But if the USSR is to remain an important power without having to rely primarily or exclusively on its military potential, some substantial changes will be required in the existing model of international relations. In the new model, no power will have the status of "superpower." A superpower is one that is able to enforce its will without regard to a larger number of independent participants in the international arena, with the result that there can be only one, or at the most two, such powers that have "divided the world." In the new model there would have to be a number of powers, but they would be dependent on each other and have no prospect of attaining superpower status and influence against the will and interests of the others.

In that case, the USSR would remain a power, together with the United States, China, the European Community, Japan, and, in time, other newly developing powers), but only on the condition that there would be cooperation among all the power centers in the international system. Armed conflict would, of course, upset this model, even if such conflict were to break out directly between just two or three of the powers. Such a model, in my view, is not unrealistic, but it is a long way from existing at present. What does exist is the danger that military conflict could destroy the entire international system. Yet even this negative element in the new outlook can provide the starting point for further positive elements—as is already happening through the negotiations on armaments.

Should this process really make headway, the "new thinking" within the USSR will still have to face a crucial conflict with Soviet society itself. The struggle will occur mainly within the power elite, but also in the consciousness of people imbued with "Great Russian" ideas. The transition to the new model for the international system will, indeed, demand a genuine, and not merely superficial and "tactical," break with everything that in both traditional thinking and prevalent ideology has generated imperialist and hegemonic ideas.

Now, as the "new thinking" begins to take shape, it is already obvious that the process involved will be difficult and contradictory. Even the present advance of glasnost, and of critical analyses of the Stalin era in particular, one can observe the cautious way in which answers to all the "sensitive questions" concerned with building up the "Soviet empire" are bypassed, or simply falsified in the old style. The forcible suppression of nationality problems after the revolution, Stalin's annexation policy in the cases of Poland and the Baltic states in 1939, the military interventions in Hungary in 1956 and Czechoslovakia in 1968— all these matters remain on the fringes of critical analysis. When pressure grows for a new critical assessment of Russian-Soviet imperial policies (as in Estonia, Latvia, and Lithuania), political tension results. In explaining the official reluctance to deal with these issues, it is frequently suggested that the truth about these matters could present a "danger to the state" and, of course, to perestroika as a whole.

Unfortunately, this line of argument is not entirely unrealistic. But that in itself indicates how far the USSR must yet go before the principles of the "new thinking" can be realized, not only in the outside world but also within Soviet society itself.

The Impact of Reform on the Soviet Bloc

After an interval of more than twenty years—since Khrushchev's downfall in 1964—moves for reform are again taking place in the "mother country" itself, the USSR, and not on the periphery of the Soviet bloc (as in Czechoslovakia in 1968). Previous experience has shown that developments in the USSR are likely to spread sooner or later to other countries in the bloc—that is, to the members of the Warsaw Pact. It is therefore appropriate to ask what importance the Gorbachev reform program may have for developments in these countries.

The situation reveals two underlying trends that are somewhat in opposition. On the one hand, the new Soviet leadership constantly emphasizes the principle of "non-interference in the internal affairs" of other members in the bloc; it strongly reiterates the right of every country to its "special road to socialism"; it renounces the claim to "absolute truth" and the role as judge of what is and what is not "the universally binding model of socialism." On the other hand, the leadership has not yet ventured a critical look at the past, when and with what consequences these principles were violated by imperialist policies. In countries where the victims of Soviet hegemony have resisted (in Yugoslavia and primarily China), there is talk of "past mistakes" on the Soviet side, too; but even in these cases no thorough analysis of the imperialistic hegemonic policies of the USSR has been undertaken. Where force has been used to suppress attempts to follow an independent course (Hungary in 1956, Czechoslovakia in 1968), the matter is passed over in silence. But when a past event becomes an immediate political issue (as happened during the twentieth anniversary of the "Prague Spring"), Soviet propaganda repeats the old politically opportune lies about the need to "defend socialism" by military intervention.

The crucial question here concerns the nature of the Soviet bloc (Warsaw Pact) as a grouping of countries having "limited sovereignty" according to the so-called Brezhnev doctrine. Membership of the bloc has hitherto meant much more than accepting the undertakings contained in the Pact (i.e., joint defense in the case of an external attack). Indeed, membership has meant an obligation to maintain an economic, political, and social system of the Soviet type. For the USSR, the real guarantee of alliance is an internal political system where, above all, the Communist party holds a monopoly of power regardless of the consensus in the society it rules. The Soviet leadership thus assumed the right to judge, in the name of "alliance and internationalism," whether internal events were likely to threaten the "common interests" of all member states. If the conclusion was that these interests were in fact threatened, they felt justified in making an armed intervention and in setting up a government to their liking without regard for the wishes of the people in the occupied country (again, as in Hungary and Czechoslovakia). Similar reasoning lay behind an alternative course—that is, use of the country's own army and police to suppress movements endeavoring to change the system by military dictatorship, as in Poland in 1981.

Any genuine reform program in the European countries of the Soviet bloc would be bound, sooner or later, to change their internal regimes. Economic and political reforms would move them away from the Soviet model, in line with their own historical traditions and special conditions. However, if the USSR sees such developments as threatening to its interests or security, and if it fails to allow the necessary degree of autonomy and tries to suppress independent developments by force, it will be unable to agree to any real guarantees for the smaller members of the bloc to go their own way. Of course, this elementary truth has always been concealed in Soviet ideology. It is concealed when one says of the Soviet bloc that "history has never known such a community of countries where no one has or can have special rights or privileges" and where everything proceeds in harmonious accord and brotherhood.[74] But a different ideological view, dating from the time of the cold war, can still be found in the West. According to this view, the Soviet use of naked force by the military and police has dominated developments in the Soviet-bloc countries from 1945 to this day. Were it not for the Soviet army, there would be prosperous Western-type democracies in these lands.

The reality differs substantially from both these ideological interpretations, and that goes for the past as well as the present.[75] Limited space precludes even a brief analysis of the history of the Soviet bloc. Let it be noted, simply, that there were two phases: During the first, roughly up to 1947–1948, events were shaped not only by external Soviet influence but also by a number of internal conflicts and anti-capitalist social forces; the second, from 1948, can be regarded as a period of outright Sovietization, with direct export of the Soviet-type system to these members of this bloc. In addition, there are considerable differences among these countries. Whereas one can imagine without difficulty a successful Western-type democracy in Czechoslovakia or the German Democratic Republic, Bulgaria or Romania, without Sovietization, would tend to move toward something similar to the situation in Turkey or Greece.

Nor is there any evidence to prove that had it not been for the strong arm of the Soviet military and police, government by the Communist parties would inevitably have broken down in all the Soviet-bloc countries, and the outcome would have been political pluralism plus the restoration of capitalism in the economy. Yugoslavia and Albania broke away from the Soviet bloc and yet moved in a different direction. And the relative independence of Ceausescu's dictatorship in Romania today plays only a reactionary role.

However, the character of the Soviet bloc, which has thus far been an association of states under the hegemony (even in their domestic affairs) of a single center based in Moscow, has not been purely the result of historical factors; some features inherent in the Soviet system have also played a part. I do not believe that this latter detail points to an inherent aggressivity in the system. True, the system is capable of aggression. That has been demonstrated many times, especially since 1939. Yet if aggression were inherent in the system, without aggression it could not successfully reproduce, strengthen, and stabilize itself—and this is clearly incorrect.

The need for hegemonic control from a single power center over groups of allied countries has arisen, in my view, from another need that is inherent in the system—namely, the need to prevent any social groupings under its rule from having autonomy, to restrict them to the extent that the power center would not be prevented from carrying out decisions, to exert total control over any movement in society. For such control is, after all, necessary for the effective operation by a system so centralized and so autocratic as the Soviet system has been.

In the context of relations with other countries, this inherent tendency can give rise to aggressive acts such as military intervention. But such intervention has occurred with respect to friendly countries that the Soviet holders of power have regarded as being in their unchallenged "sphere of influence"—an area over which they could have total control. Where rival systems (such as the "capitalist world") are concerned, the Soviet leadership has not aimed at total control; thus its actions have not necessarily led to aggression in these cases, even when there have been conflicts of interest.

If this interpretation of the factors that have shaped relations between the USSR and members of the Soviet bloc is correct, than one cannot theoretically dismiss the possibility that these relations may change in the future to the extent that the process of management and control within the Soviet system comes to differ from the primitive model based on commands and prohibitions issued from a single center. In other words, should the attempt at radical reform of the economic and political system in the USSR be successful, should the power center cease to govern society by commands that assume the recipients have been deprived of the possibility to act independently, and should it start to rule by indirect methods, the present nature of relations among the Soviet-bloc states would likely change in time. Indeed, a move toward greater autonomy and sovereignty could be the result.

However, this is a hypothesis for the long term. As yet, I cannot back it up by pointing to any actual radical changes. There are definite reasons for the caution exhibited by the Soviet leadership in its relations with the other countries in the bloc. First, the leadership is at present fully occupied with domestic problems, and with contentious relations in various parts of the world (from the United States to China). There is also past experience, as when Khrushchev's attempt to launch an open revision of relations with the countries in the bloc led to "events" in Poland and Hungary in the fall of 1956, with political consequences that threatened the position of Khrushchev himself and caused the slowing down of the reform program in the USSR.

Moreover, the longer Soviet hegemony persists in its present form, the greater will be the resistance to "alliance with the USSR." Moves toward reforming relations will also become more difficult. Especially in the countries where attempts at taking an independent course were suppressed fairly recently (Czechoslovakia and especially Poland), the political situation has undergone marked polarization, and the outlook for peaceful and gradual reform is less promising than before the reform attempts were suppressed.

All in all, the new Soviet leadership has good cause to proceed with great caution. Probably only when it has strengthened its position in other areas will it change its practice and allow greater autonomy for the smaller members of the bloc. In the long term, however, one can expect that success with the reform in the USSR will lead to changes in these relations as well.

The nature of such changes is controversial, however, and some ideas occasionally advanced in the West can hardly be regarded as realistic. The proposals for "Finlandization" of the European countries in the Soviet bloc fall in this category. These ideas stem from the view that the interests of USSR security would be sufficiently safeguarded by an otherwise completely open political and economic development in these countries, roughly on the model of Finland.[76]

In my view "Finlandization" might have been possible for some of these countries after 1945, but not after forty years of Sovietization. The obstacle is by no means solely the USSR and its interests; it is also the whole economic, social, and political situation in the Soviet-bloc countries that are "proposed" for Finlandization.

Regarding the interests of the USSR, three circumstances are significant: First, the neutrality of Finland, in view of its geographical position and its population, suits the interests of the USSR as a great power. But that cannot be said of the whole complex of countries in the Warsaw Pact, which represent altogether some 100 million people (i.e., nearly one-third of the entire population of the "socialist community") and which, for forty years have been subordinate states (with not inconsiderable armies). Its great power interests could hardly allow the USSR to renounce its immediate ties of alliance—at least not for the foreseeable future, given the political situation in Europe as it is today.

Second, the states currently in the Soviet bloc represent an economic factor for the USSR that can scarcely be excluded from the drive to modernize the Soviet economy. The whole reform program, and the transition of the economy to intensive development, is logically conceived as a program embracing the economic capacities of the other bloc members. Further economic integration within the Comecon framework is an essential element in the Soviet plans.

Third, there is a serious ideological and political reason for the inapplicability of the "Finlandization" model. The maxim about the so-called irreversibility of socialism (in Soviet ideological terminology, "the inadmissibility of counter-revolution and the restoration of capitalism") has much more than just ideological significance. It has been the basis for Soviet power in the USSR itself throughout its history. The way out of this vicious circle for European development is to recognize "special roads to socialism" for different countries, not to renounce the postulates about "irreversible development" in the Soviet-bloc countries. Insofar as there is justification in the West for demanding that the stand on irreversible development should be revised as the condition for stable peace and a new order in Europe,[77] one can see such a revision as feasible only on the lines outlined above. In a sense, the model would be Yugoslavia rather than Finland.

From the standpoint of the smaller Soviet-bloc members, the following factors would speak against applying the Finlandization model: After forty years of Sovietization, none of these countries would be capable, without serious internal crises and upheavals, of independent existence once their vital ties with the USSR and Comecon were broken. Living standards (though constantly subject to criticism) and social security could not be maintained in any of these countries if they were suddenly to be exposed to pressure from world markets; their economic backwardness (e.g., their inability to compete) would have serious consequences.

A number of expert works have been written on the subject of Soviet-bloc economic problems, including one regarding the implications of the reform program.[78] In brief, it may be said that for the East-bloc countries forty years of Soviet hegemony have meant isolation from world markets, economies distorted to fit the Soviet economy and its requirements, and the countries' inability to exist economically as sovereign states. They are crippled actors in the world economy for whom today's verbal guarantee of "independent, special development" has come too late— even if it is meant seriously and is guaranteed by the Soviets.

This is true not only for the countries that were once economically advanced (especially Czechoslovakia and the GDR) but also for those where Soviet-type industrialization involved a switch from a backward agrarian structure to extensive industrial development (Romania, Bulgaria, Poland, and to a lesser extent Hungary). Even this industrial advance was of a quality and a form that have resulted in today's economic backwardness and one-sided dependence on the USSR, and in the inability to compete on the world market as independent industrial partners. In the case of the countries that were previously advanced and, at the start of Sovietization (around 1948), were able to compete with Western European countries and were also at the same level of technological advance (Czechoslovakia and the GDR), there has been evident degeneration and a loss of the competitiveness that once existed.

The negative role played by the USSR's hegemony over the smaller Soviet-bloc countries lies in these circumstances rather than in direct "economic exploitation," unfavorable prices, and so on. For this reason, Comecon as a means for integration, originally intended to ensure political advantage, never became an instrument for integrating these countries into the world economy. On the contrary, it became a form of collective isolation from the world market, such that they fell behind the economic and technological development in the advanced industrial countries. That situation is radically different from that of postwar Finland and of Austria in 1955.

I believe that for the economic reasons mentioned here, Finlandization does not offer a way out. The only course is one that the Soviet-bloc countries will have to take as a whole while maintaining their close economic ties. In time, these ties will change from being instruments for ensuring Soviet hegemony into instruments of beneficial cooperation between East and West Europe—that is, between the EEC and Comecon and, within this framework of bilateral contacts, between 'different countries.

Politically, the present situation in the bloc is extremely complicated. Some trends are common to all the smaller countries, and others are very diverse and specific to individual countries. Among the common trends is the longing of nations for independence and sovereign status. These aspirations often reach beyond the reality of the world today, beyond any realistic political possibilities; they overlook the fact that, in view of the irreversible integration processes in the world, some measure of dependence (especially economic) is simply a fact for smaller countries everywhere. There is simply no escape from it.

In a free plebiscite (which is not a practical proposition), I believe an enormous majority (maybe 70 to 80 percent) in countries such as Czechoslovakia, Hungary, and Poland would vote for neutrality or withdrawal from the bloc. This is probable also in the GDR, where a strong trend toward the unification of Germany would be evident as well.

This leaning toward neutrality, and the growing consciousness among the Soviet-bloc countries of "belonging to Europe" (often voiced as a call for recognizing "Central Europe" in contrast to Eastern Europe) is, in the final analysis, an expression of efforts to break away from Soviet hegemony, to seek an opportunity for autonomous existence in a sovereign national state. This strong desire to be a part of Europe is not matched by the actual ability of either the ruling circles or the populations to integrate economically, politically, and nationally in Europe as it stands today. After all, West European integration is suffering from a whole range of economic, political, and national conflicts that will take a long time to resolve. The Sovietized part of Europe, however, is an area where the economic, political, and national structure will have to undergo a lengthy and complicated process before it can reach a degree of integration comparable to that of Western Europe today.

The political situation in the European countries of the Soviet bloc reveals an exceptional diversity that was lacking only a few years ago. For a variety of reasons, the outcome is the same in almost all of these countries: The political leaderships in the majority declare themselves for perestroika, but in reality their aim is to maintain their own positions and the stability of their regimes. In short, they wish to change as little as possible. This is true of the GDR, Czechoslovakia, and Bulgaria. Romania which maintains a Stalinist-type dictatorship, is a case apart.

In Hungary and Poland, the support for Gorbachev's policies holds out little promise. Granted, there is some support in Hungary for economic reform and certain political reforms that can be seen as a kind of small-scale experimental test for Gorbachev's ideas. At the same time, however, Hungary is experiencing something of a crisis in its current reform program. Resolution of this crisis would mean going further in terms of both economic measures and radical political democratization. Indeed, the new situation calls for measures going beyond the framework of the Gorbachev program, especially given that in its political culture, ideas about political pluralism, and so on, Hungary is historically more influenced than Russia by Western traditions. Following Kadar's departure and the succession of the new political leadership the situation in Hungary has become, in a sense, similar to the Prague Spring in Czechoslovakia in 1968. The younger generations are no longer influenced by the suppression of the revolution in 1956; moreover, the prevailing view is that Moscow under Gorbachev presents no threat to a radical reform program. However, if the course taken becomes too radical—especially given the moves being made toward political pluralism and the fact that the country is presented in the USSR as a "model" for reform—the result could be a strengthening of militant anti-reform forces in the USSR that would force Gorbachev to distance himself from events in Hungary. The political leaderships in Czechoslovakia, the GDR, Bulgaria, and Romania could also exert pressure on Gorbachev in this respect.

The Polish leadership too eagerly supports Soviet reform policies and seeks to find a way out of its crisis along that road. But General Wojciech Jaruzelski's Poland is not really an unqualified supporter of the Gorbachev course; rather, it is a potential danger to reform in the USSR and throughout the Soviet bloc. Poland's power structure has already relied for some years on armed force—on an army and a police system that proved capable of standing up to the mass movement of Solidarity with the help of martial law in 1981. The Communist party's political authority and effective capacity to act are almost nil. Hence the declared reform policy there is of negligible importance. The gulf between the majority of the population and the political power holders has not been bridged, even seven years after "resolving the crisis" by means of martial law. The economic crisis drags on, with little chance of ending without economic aid from the United States. The social situation is fluid and continues to be potentially explosive. Politically, given the existing state of affairs between government (the armed forces) and an opposition obliged to exist illegally (Solidarity), the main force in the land is the Roman Catholic Church, which has no chance of achieving a political solution. The reforms required by the crisis in Poland (and desired by a majority of the public) are different in nature from those launched by Gorbachev in the USSR. A majority consensus for reform policies is hardly possible in Poland without genuine power sharing with the opposition. But the military government in Poland has been able to lay claim to legitimacy precisely because it has maintained the monopoly of a single party by force. So now it can scarcely break that monopoly without serious consequences for itself. Yet in the long term there is no other way. The search for viable compromises that could lead toward that end will be fraught with difficulty.

The present leadership under Jaruzelski hopes that Gorbachev will "permit" reform to end the crisis and that there will be no threat of Soviet military intervention to stop it. For the same reasons (hope that Gorbachev will permit reforms) the population is generally supportive of Gorbachev. At the same time, however, the radical opposition sees the Soviet reforms as heralding the "break-up" of the Soviet empire. It also hopes that Poland will ultimately gain complete independence from the USSR.

We need hardly emphasize that this ambiguous "support for Gorbachev" is, from the Soviet standpoint, even more dangerous than in the case of Hungary. For the situation in Poland is potentially explosive.[79] A confrontation between society and the power holders could occur at any time, as in 1981, and that would deal a severe blow to the reform movements both in the USSR and throughout the Soviet bloc.

Thus, the leadership in two out of the six countries in the Soviet bloc that support Gorbachev in the hope that the reform policies will help to solve their own problems are at the same time on the verge of economic crisis and facing an uncertain political situation. In the remaining four countries the conservative leadership either pays lip service to Gorbachev's reforms or (in the case of Romania and the GDR) expresses serious reservations concerning his policies. Only one of them—Romania—is faced with a potentially explosive situation. The present state of affairs in Romania is due in part to its many years of relative independence from policies in the USSR and the bloc as a whole. Regardless of what happens in Romania in the way of internal conflicts, it is unlikely either to pose a threat to the Gorbachev leadership in Moscow or to affect the rest of the bloc. In the event of disturbance, Romania will be largely isolated.

The remaining three countries—Bulgaria, the GDR, and Czechoslovakia—are relics of the Brezhnev era, but there seems little danger of mass unrest. Their leaderships have adopted a conservative wait-and-see attitude and, at times, an openly critical stance toward some aspects of Gorbachev's program. Indeed, outward "peace and prosperity" reigns in all these countries, albeit in the guise of political inertia among the majority of the population and with economies stagnating, though not in crisis.

The least worrisome situation among these three countries is that in Bulgaria. The leadership there does not express opposition but, rather, tries—as always—to follow the Soviet line while firmly maintaining personal continuity (in the person of Todor Zhivkov) and with a clear emphasis on initiative "from above."

The leadership in the GDR openly defends its "own road." It resists any moves to "copy the USSR" and to adopt all aspects of perestroika, especially in relation to political reform, glasnost, and criticism of the past (i.e., criticism of both the Stalin and Brezhnev periods). According to the GDR leadership, the necessary basic reforms, especially in the economy, were carried out long before Gorbachev's time. Their main argument concerns the relative viability of the economic system. But this relative prosperity of the GDR cannot be divorced from several special factors, including the "German-German" relations that enable the GDR to share in some of the advantages enjoyed by the Western EEC economies. Political democratization in the GDR would certainly follow a different course from that in Russia; among other things, it would open up the "German question." For all these reasons the present attitude of the GDR leadership is more acceptable over the short haul than any risky experiments that might emerge in that country.

The situation in Czechoslovakia is unique. Twenty years ago, during the Prague Spring of 1968, a short-lived attempt was made to reform the economic and political systems. This effort had many basic features in common with today's perestroika.[80] The command system of economic planning was to be replaced by a system relying on economic factors that linked the plan with the market in order to move from extensive to intensive growth. The economic reform was linked to political reform based on democratization, which entails freedom of criticism and opinion, freedom of the press, transformation of the state into one based on the rule of law, self-government in socialist enterprises, internal reform of the ruling Communist party, establishment of institutional opportunities for social control over the party, and subordination of the party apparatus to democratic control.

However, the political line of the reform communists, declared by Moscow, Warsaw, and Berlin to be counterrevolutionary, was suppressed by the military intervention of August 1968. What followed were twenty years of "normalization"—forcible restoration of the Soviet-type system in its post-Stalin/Brezhnev form. A fundamental political change thus occurred in Czechoslovakia; mainly because normalization bred and consolidated public distrust in the ability of the rulers genuinely to link socialism and democracy—that is, to democratize and radically change the Soviet-type system. Moreover, anti-Soviet and anti-Russian feelings, which had previously been quite negligible in Czechoslovakia, now spread. Entire generations came to regard the USSR as an occupation power. A forcible purge in the Communist party (roughly one-third of the membership was removed in 1970) wiped out the very democratic potential that might have enabled it to carry out on its own initiative a policy of democratization and reform "from above," drawing on the country's situation prior to the enforced Stalinization of 1948.

All this has politically crippled Czechoslovakia; its actions as a state, its society, and its national Communist party have all been affected. Gorbachev's calls for independence—his declarations about the right of every country to follow its own path—have a particularly hollow ring here because, for decades, all the factors making such independence possible were suppressed by the Soviets. Therefore, if the new Soviet leadership confines itself to these general declarations and does nothing to help overcome the consequences of coercive actions by its own predecessors, the current perestroika policy will be profoundly discredited in the eyes of the Czechoslovak people. They are still waiting passively, for they see little purpose in working actively for reform and democratization. They see no guarantee from the Soviet leadership that attempts at democratization will not be met once again by suppression and revenge.

In general, then, Soviet perestroika is having a diverse impact in the bloc. The situation now is very different from that of 1956. Then Khrushchev's "de-Stalinization" was a signal for all the countries to follow suit; and because measures far more radical than those in the USSR were quickly undertaken in the smaller European countries (the GDR, Poland, and Hungary) in the form of pressure "from below," the events in Poland and Hungary severely shook

Khrushchev's position. Today Gorbachev is more likely to face the danger that perestroika will be discredited in the smaller countries of the bloc, given the persistence of passive wait-and-see attitudes. The cautious tactics displayed by the new Soviet leadership toward individual members of the bloc, which want "calm" rather than risky ventures, have led the people in the bloc countries to view the policy not as an attempt to democratize life in their countries but as an effort to maintain the existing groups in power—those that are "pro-Moscow" under all circumstances.

The Gorbachev leadership seems to lack as yet any clearly thought out policy for relations with the bloc—just as it still lacks any coherent approach to the nationality question within the USSR itself. Gorbachev has repeatedly proclaimed a number of principles, especially the right of each country to its own special development, independence for every Communist party, the fact that the CPSU does not wish to impose the Soviet model on anyone else, and so on. But he has also chosen not to disassociate himself in straightforward, politically convincing terms from the past infringements of these principles by the USSR.

Even the current approach to relations with the Soviet-bloc countries is very contradictory: Slogans about independence contrast with the increasing tendency toward uniform action and the steps being taken toward integration at the level of individual enterprises that are not economically justified and are carried out in an administrative manner reminiscent of the old Stalinist "mixed concerns," which damaged the economies concerned and subjected them to Soviet hegemony. In the political sphere there are frequent meetings to which leading figures from the Warsaw Pact countries are summoned—a practice that appears to be an attempt to support the groups now in power, rather than to encourage democratization and a movement for reform in the smaller countries of the bloc.

The crux of the matter, on the one hand, is that the Soviet leadership is aware that reform and democratization in the smaller countries will again proceed, if the way is open to them, in directions and at a pace different from that in the USSR. They are evidently conscious of the fact that historical traditions and influences not present in Russian political culture will again be strongly felt. They also know that moves for independence from Moscow will not be lacking. On the other hand, the leadership has no clear idea as to what it wants and can tolerate in this connection, and what it does not want and cannot allow. It is not sure what would happen if military force (i.e., the presence of Soviet troops) actually ceased holding together the "socialist fraternal community" in the Warsaw Pact and Comecon. Consequently, the leadership proceeds pragmatically, leaving free rein for "independent roads" in different countries, but in fact merely helping to maintain matters as they existed under Brezhnev. Then, when there is an actual crisis, as in Poland and Romania, it avoids taking responsibility for what may happen. In reality, the nature of the Soviet bloc as a grouping of states with "limited sovereignty" is not changed. Nor is there any change in the role of military power and Soviet hegemony in the bloc, although hegemony is incapable of offering these smaller countries the progress they desire.

If these problems are not tackled in time and in a new way, the very endeavor to "keep things calm" may evoke unrest in some of the countries. In 1956, after all, the cause of the events in Poland and Hungary was that the old Stalinists tried to maintain themselves in power and to impose themselves on the public as the guarantors of a new policy. It was not that the leaders in those countries were overhasty in making radical changes.

The key question is whether the USSR will be able to transform the bloc into an alliance of sovereign states that, while remaining dependent on each other (for the economic reasons already mentioned), are not forced from a single center to maintain identical political systems but, rather, can evolve in quite diverse directions in accordance with their different historical traditions and potentials. They cannot continue to be occupied by Soviet troops. Their economic integration must rely on economic efficiency and mutual advantage, and not be dominated by the needs and planning procedures of the USSR.

Naturally, these aims can be achieved only through compromise. The idea that individual countries can take unilateral action to free themselves from the web of economic and political dependence is an impracticable one. The USSR but also the Western powers—from the United States to Britain, France, and West Germany—would not risk upheavals in Europe because of such attempts by individual countries in the Soviet bloc. Therefore, I believe the only realistic course is that the bloc should proceed as a whole in gradually changing its existing situation, while maintaining close economic and political ties among the member countries. This process will be a lengthy one, lasting for at least a decade.

Meanwhile, in the best case, cooperative relations could also develop between Eastern and Western Europe, including bilateral cooperation between countries from both sides. The prospect of all-European integration is not yet a practical proposition. I believe it is conceivable in the long term, however, that progress will be made away from the existing structural model whereby political and military blocs confront each other in Europe. Toward this end, the Soviet bloc will need to find positive solutions to two main sets of problems involving the military character of the USSR as a power and the limited sovereignty of the smaller states in the Warsaw Pact. On the solution of these problems will depend the effectiveness of the instruments and methods that have in recent years developed in European politics.

I have in mind primarily the development of bilateral and multilateral relations among European countries irrespective of the blocs they belong to, as was the case during the Helsinki process. This process involved both contacts that increased mutual confidence (including steps to resolve certain military questions) and relations of cooperation in the economic and cultural areas.

Undoubtedly the Helsinki process created a new and more positive situation, mainly with respect to regional matters in Europe. For instance, relations between West and East Germany are today not only more positive but also relatively less dependent on the immediate bipolar conflict between the superpowers than in the years before the West German Socialists' Ostpolitik was launched. The neutral and nonaligned countries in Europe as a whole have come to play a greater role. Some regional relationships (e.g., between Austria and Hungary) offer quite a good example for a cooperative model of East-West relations.

Accordingly, the instruments and methods already created and applied in the Helsinki process—if they continue to be used—can be seen as offering one means of superseding the bloc model in Europe. A big contribution would be made if results could soon be achieved in some of the negotiations that have been under way for years with no practical outcome. I have in mind especially the negotiations on reducing conventional forces in Central Europe. With military disengagement between the blocs on European territory, zones free of nuclear and chemical weapons established, and so on, the present bloc model of relations in Europe could be politically superseded. Similarly, every real advance, in both economic and cultural cooperation, would work toward this end.

It is important that we realize, however, that if change takes place in two main problems—the USSR as a super-power in the military sense alone, and the nature of the Soviet bloc—the instruments and methods for bringing about political relaxation will be of only limited value. To the extent that these problems remain unresolved—and their solution, of course, depends on developments within the Soviet-type systems—not much more can be gained from political steps to reduce tension than has been achieved in recent years. In particular, there will be no escape from the blind alley created by the strategy of deterrence based on military strength.

If, on the other hand, the USSR changes its nature as a power and the Soviet bloc assumes a new character, the instruments and methods for political relaxation would immediately acquire new importance, and new opportunities for using them would arise. The road toward that objective will be very complicated and precarious—and certainly not short. I believe, however, that it is a road that can be followed.

Postscript: The Problems of the Soviet Reforms in 1989

Political developments in the USSR are taking place so rapidly that even a few months can be of crucial significance; comments based on the situation in 1988 can easily be outdated in 1989. This book was conceived and written around the time of the 19th CPSU All-Union Conference in the summer of 1988, and the final version of the manuscript was edited in the autumn of that year. By the time it went to press, certain trends had become clearer. They are discussed briefly in this postscript written in April 1989.

I believe that at least a few words are needed to highlight certain new trends, especially in connection with the following groups of problems: (1) economic policy (above all, agricultural policy), (2) practical experiences revealed by the elections to the soviets at the end of March 1989, (3) the national question, (4) developments in certain smaller Soviet-bloc countries (especially in Poland and Hungary), and (5) East-West relations after the U.S. presidential elections in November 1988.

A detailed analysis of these problems is not possible, of course. It would require at least one more chapter of a work that is already completed. Hence I shall make only a few brief remarks.

The reform policy can triumph in the economic sphere only if, by the time of a further decisive confrontation between the reform and anti-reform forces (roughly by 1990–1991), at least certain marginal successes have been achieved, bringing average citizens at least some improvements in their material living standards. Under Soviet conditions this will entail solutions to the flagrant shortages (and rationing "on coupons") of basic foodstuffs, at least in the greater part of the USSR, improvements in basic services and social care, and improvements in the critical housing situation (especially for young couples). We needn't expect miracles in the form of Western-style satisfaction of consumer needs. There are no guarantees of such satisfaction in the USSR; if anything, present developments have worsened the conditions of the majority of the population, especially those of the socially weakest sections.

The reasons underlying these circumstances are rather complicated, but in general one can attribute them to the fact that the old command system of economic management is no longer working, whereas the new method of management based on market mechanisms is still far from functioning. Public discussions are increasingly characterized by sharp conflicts of views—couched, for the moment, in general theoretical terms. Is it possible or not to ensure that the market mechanism will soon work satisfactorily? Does the USSR have not only the technical and economic but also the social prerequisites for this mechanism? Leonid I. Abalkin, a foremost Soviet economist and supporter of market reforms, is openly skeptical: In the USSR, he maintains, there is a shortage of millions of "entirely different workers" than those produced by the command system over decades. This state of affairs strengthens the tendency for a return to the old command system. Other Soviet economists take the opposite stance: They propose giving more space to market mechanisms in the consumer industry but suggest that other branches should be planned from above with the help of so-called state orders.[81] Still others imply the need for a return to the old management methods.

In its struggle for concept and pace (including ideological disputes regarding what is and what is not "socialism" in the economic sense of the word), and in its even more crucial conflicts about the form and implementation of a practical economic reform policy, the USSR still faces major problems in the sphere of economic reform. Implementation of these reforms will take place in a situation of fading euphoria, stemming from the elation caused by the possibility of being able to discuss reforms and submit proposals on them. On the contrary, skepticism will spread because neither the old system nor the new one will be able to function. That situation is not only unfavorable for the reformers but potentially dangerous as well.

Gorbachev and his leadership appear to be trying to open the way for various approaches and experiments. They do not seem to have a clear vision about the methods for arriving at the desired economic outcome. Typical examples are the conclusions of the CPSU Central Committee session devoted to agricultural policy.[82] All forms of agricultural management—from state and collective farms to land leases to farming families who work the land for a period of up to fifty years to farming by individuals on privately owned land (peasants' private plots)—are "socialist" and thus "acceptable"; they will be endorsed by the state simply in order to achieve higher production and improve supplies for the population. The priority given to certain methods of farming—especially the leasing of land (even within collective farms) to families—has been declared, but different interpretations of this decision can also easily be suppressed. The fact that the bodies administering agricultural production (down to district level) have ceased to be administrative institutions of the state, and are to be constituted as economically based associations of agricultural enterprises, is no doubt an achievement. But there is still some doubt whether all this will mean a genuine revolutionary transformation in the Soviet countryside, as now proclaimed, and a "development of the productive forces" in agriculture. The struggle for a new system of agricultural production, which may yet be won by the conservative forces, will be complex indeed.

The situation in Soviet industry is even more complex. Quite a number of vicious circles must be broken, but for the moment no one knows how this is to be done. It is clear, for example, that without a price reform (i.e., without the abolition of subsidies on unprofitable products, the introduction of economically justified prices, and so on), it will be impossible to arrive at a market mechanism for economic management. But price reform in the USSR is being postponed for the time being out of a fear of the serious social and, hence, political consequences resulting from such a reform. When and how will it be possible to break these vicious circles? Only future (and possibly conflicting) developments will provide an answer.

If the economic reform process remains in a blind alley and reform policy in this sphere surrenders to the conservatives, the overall reform—encompassing domestic politics as well as international relations—could be endangered. Yet the progress of the political reforms (democratization, glasnost, and so on) is proceeding more rapidly and more radically than originally anticipated, thus providing significant hope for a triumph of the reform forces in a conflict about economic policy. To the extent that this conflict is formulated openly and solved under public control, the defeat of the conservatives (i.e., the supporters of the Stalinist command system) is more likely than their victory.

With respect to political reform, the elections of delegates to the Congress of People's Representatives at the end of March 1989 revealed a qualitative change relative to past routine. All the critical remarks made in Chapter 2 in connection with the new electoral laws in the USSR remain valid. The key problem to be tackled is still far from being solved: True decisionmaking, on personnel questions as well as economic and political measures—must take place in institutions under public democratic control—and nowhere else. The party apparatus must therefore cease to be "a state within a state"; otherwise, no qualitative transformation of the entire political system is possible.

As the elections demonstrated, however, trends are beginning to advance in this direction. Roughly 25 to 30 percent of the constituencies elected candidates other than those preferred by the party apparatus. Moreover, the candidates backed by the apparatus were constantly confronted by arguments and debates at voters' meetings. In a number of cases, high party, state, and economic officials failed to be elected and the voters gave preference to more or less unknown candidates not supported by the apparatus. The case of Boris Yeltsin's election in Moscow was evidently a political demonstration by the electorate against the entire CPSU Central Committee, which, shortly before the elections, had begun to "investigate critically" his political activity. This official step against Yeltsin in fact increased his popularity among the voters.

In addition, the number of leading secretaries of party bodies not elected as deputies was far higher than anticipated by the party apparatus (and maybe even by the voters themselves). If the principle formulated by the 19th All-Union CPSU Conference were to be translated into reality, these people would be dismissed from their party posts. Events in the near future will show whether and to what extent this is the case.

The elections, especially in the Baltic republics (Lithuania, Latvia, Estonia), and the bloody demonstrations in Georgia early in April, have shown that the nationalities question plays (and will continue to play) a more significant role in the reform process in the USSR than I anticipated during the writing of this book. I am still of the opinion that the USSR is not doomed to disintegration as a result of nationalities conflicts. On the contrary, the reform is capable of coming to grips even with such conflicts in a multinational state. But experience has shown that a whole series of other problems (economic, political, and sociocultural) will be raised in the non-Russian territories of the USSR in direct connection with the nationalities problem. Also linked with this problem are discontent and pressure "from below," in the form of mass demonstrations and protest actions (such as strikes). In connection with the nationalities problem, demands emerge that are unacceptable to Gorbachev's pro-reform policy. I have in mind the demands being made for the secession of certain national republics from the USSR. These, as distinct from other demands that are currently unacceptable to Gorbachev (e.g., the establishment of opposition parties), would, without suppression by force, easily obtain mass support in non-Russian areas.

But the use of force in suppressing mass protest demonstration has proved to be incapable of solving conflicts accumulated over long years. This has been the case in Armenia (the problem of the region known as Nagorny Karabakh remains potentially explosive) and in Georgia (where casualties among innocent human beings have provided a glaring illustration of the absurdity of attempts to solve politically embarrassing problems by the use of force).

If a different, fundamentally democratic solution of the nationalities problem is not found in time, it could become a stumbling block for the entire reform program. Many indications suggest that the Gorbachev leadership is aware of the gravity of the nationalities problem in relation to the fate of the reform policy. Edvard Shevardnadze, in a speech about the events in Georgia, highlighted both the absolute inadmissibility of unjustified force being employed by state bodies and the damage such a procedure could cause to the overall advance of the policy of democratization as well as to the credibility of the new Soviet policy abroad.[83]

Also important are the facts that the solution of the nationalities problem cannot circumvent problems such as sovereignty (i.e., the independence and self-determination of nations), that changes must also affect the present constitutional concept of the USSR, that the Constitution itself must correspond to "the actual realities and needs and not wishful thinking" about federations as well as their nationality components, and that a federation must be based on "genuine mutual confidence among nationalities."

Even under these circumstances, the implications of the nationalities problem for the total reform policy of the USSR remain delicate and potentially explosive.

New facts relating to certain smaller Soviet-bloc states, especially Poland and Hungary, emerged early in 1989. I believe that what I wrote about this issue in the preceding chapters remains valid—but experience has shown that the swiftest development is taking place in areas exerting the strongest pressure on the regime. In Poland a dialogue between the government and the opposition mainstream has reached a crucial political compromise: Solidarity, the independent trade union organization, has again been authorized and an agreement has been reached regarding a transition period during which the representation of the opposition in parliament is guaranteed by a 35 percent share of seats. Moreover, an independent Senate is to be formed whose members will be elected in free elections without any restrictions imposed on the opposition. This Senate will have specific control rights as well as the right of veto vis-à-vis Parliament, which needs a two-thirds majority to overrule the Senate veto. This is an institutionally anchored method of ensuring a true transition toward political pluralism.

As Poland's exceedingly grave economic situation is not thereby solved, however, the possibility of further eruptive developments cannot be ruled out. But the likelihood of catastrophic conflicts has been reduced, and there are greater hopes that the political power will be capable of achieving what it failed to achieve in 1981—a qualitative transformation of the entire management system.

In Hungary, whose situation has been likened to the "Prague Spring" of 1968, developments are likewise proceeding along a road of radical and speedy political reforms. Pluralism of interests has been guaranteed institutionally by new rules on the right of assembly, and the emergence of new political parties has been admitted in principle. It is likely that this process will lead to a coalition government of several parties (although its actual form has not yet been determined).

The radical development of the political system in two Soviet-bloc countries has naturally affected the situation in the other states of the bloc. In Czechoslovakia and the GDR, especially, the leaderships are finding it increasingly difficult to maintain a basically unchanged political situation. The Hungarian and Polish developments are providing a new impetus to developments in the USSR even though certain aspects of these developments are unrealistic for Gorbachev's concept of reform in the USSR.

Increasingly voiced in connection with these trends in the Soviet bloc is the opinion that, for countries such as Hungary, neutrality could be a realistic prospect. I refer here to a kind of "Finlandization" in the political and socioeconomic sense. This opinion was expressed, for example, by the foremost Soviet scholar Oleg Bogomolov during his recent visit to Hungary.[84] I believe that a discussion of this issue is both possible and necessary, but I am personally of the following opinion, expounded in greater detail in the preceding chapters of this book: After forty years of Soviet hegemony, the further development of the Warsaw Treaty and the Comecon countries is conceivable only as a joint experience based on new (economic and political) foundations of East European integration; and only in this context is there a realistic prospect of cooperation with an integrated West European entity, of bilateral cooperation among individual West and East European countries, and regional development of Central Europe beyond the borders of the bloc. In the long term (around the year 2000), it will be possible to speak also of other prospects for Europe as a whole.

But the realization of these prospects will depend, in the final analysis, on whether and to what extent Gorbachev's foreign policy succeeds in bringing about global changes in the system of international relations. Indeed, can it overcome a situation in which the military plays the decisive role, while also surmounting the existing bipolar model of the world? Toward this end, the present role of the superpowers would have to be abolished and a truly functional polycentrist system of international relations would have to be created.

The developments of 1989 contributed no real advances in this direction, especially from the West. In his speech to the UN General Assembly, Gorbachev probably went as far as the Soviet leadership is able to go unilaterally in revising the existing Soviet concept of international relations and further disarmament, but without claiming countermeasures from the West, particularly the United States.[85] In a sense, his speech can be seen as a kind of practical framework offered to President George Bush prior to the latter's access to office on 20 January 1989.

The Soviet leadership has not been satisfied with the response from the new U.S. administration, as Gorbachev made fairly clear during his visit to Britain in April 1989.[86] The main reason for this dissatisfaction is the fact that, in U.S. foreign policy, a stronger tendency than in the past is beginning to emerge calling for passivity and marking time rather than for taking the initiative at a time when international relations are undergoing change. This tendency can be summed up as follows: (1) Gorbachev's perestroika is a risky business, and its defeat may not be far away. (2) In international East-West relations, the United States must wait and see how far the new Soviet policy will go in taking its practical unilateral steps. (3) The "new political thinking" (i.e., Gorbachev's repeatedly stated view that war, including even conventional war, has ceased to be a feasible instrument of politics) belongs in the realm of utopian ideology, or even propaganda. (4) Only the present policy of deterrence ("a balance of fear") can continue to serve as the basis for Western policy toward the USSR. And (5) in relations with other communist governments (from China to Yugoslavia and Poland), the United States must differentiate on the basis of the policy of each, acting always in accordance with the principle of "quid pro quo."

There are surely many reasons for each of these contentions; they cannot simply be brushed aside when viewed from the standpoint of the ruling circles in the West. But together these attitudes constitute, in my opinion, a basically bureaucratic reaction to a new historical situation brought about by the policy of perestroika, not only in the USSR but throughout the world. I describe this reaction as bureaucratic because it clings to the status quo and risks nothing in the way of real change in foreign policy and military affairs.

If such bureaucratic reaction were really to determine the foreign policy of the West, the consequences would, in my opinion, be extremely negative as well as dangerous. The "new political thinking" in the USSR means the possibility of qualitatively different behavior by the entire Soviet bloc. But if it is defeated by bureaucratic, negative, and passive reactions on the part of the West, it will inevitably be replaced by some form of offensive militarism.

And this would surely not be in the interest of either the East or the West. Indeed, the ultimate outcome would be catastrophe, rather than victory, for all of the parties in the worldwide feud.

Personally I do not believe that such a catastrophic outcome is likely. In spite of the not exactly encouraging situation at the beginning of 1989, I believe that the overall tendencies for the development of East-West relations remain positive. I simply cannot accept the thesis that the West is unable to influence the fate of the new Soviet policy. On the contrary, such influence—whether it proceeds from passivity or activity on the part of the West—is quite likely. Let us hope that it contributes to the success and not to the defeat of the domestic and world processes to which this book is devoted.

Notes

1. For comprehensive data, surveys, and analyses of economic matters, see, e.g., *The Soviet Union 1986/1987*, edited by the Federal Institute for East European and International Studies in Cologne (Boulder: Westview Press 1989), section on "The Economy," pp. 101–192. The following subjects are dealt with, including references to sources and other works: Hans-Hermann Höhmann: The Soviet Economy Under Gorbachev: In Search of a New Profile; Hermann Clement: The Restructuring of Soviet Investment and Structural Policy; Hans-Henning Schröder: Arms and the USSR's Economy Under Gorbachev; Eberhart Schinke: Problems of Development and Chances for Consolidation in Soviet Agriculture; Gertraud Seidenstecher: Consumption Policy Under Gorbachev: More Material Incentives—But How?; Roland Götz-Coenenberg: Approaches to and Problems with Soviet System Policy Under Gorbachev (Organizational and Planning Reforms); Christian Meyer: New Directions in Soviet Foreign Trade. For critical analyses from left positions of economic aspects of soviet reform policies, see articles by Hansgeorg Conert in the journal *Sozialismus* (VSA-Verlag Hamburg), 1985–1988.

2. Differences in the historical backgrounds and developments among the European countries of the Soviet bloc are analyzed in greater detail in Jürgen Hartmann, *Politik und Gesellschaft in Osteuropa* (Frankfurt and New York: Campus, 1983), p. 280. See also Jens Hacker, *Der Ostblock: Entstehung, Entwicklung und Struktur* (Baden-Baden: Nomos Verlag, 1983), p. 1045. This work provides a number of facts, but the analysis and evaluation are often one-sided and subjective.

3. In this connection, the Soviet press published in 1987–1988 many complaints about the reluctance of kolkhoz members to take advantage of the independence offered to them, and about the lack of infrastructure (e.g., inadequate transportation for goods destined for the free market). The radical proposals

announced by Gorbachev in October 1988 for giving the peasants a stake in the land by leasing farm holdings may gradually bring a change for the better, although such radical ideas are bound to meet with distrust among generations whose experience with the system has been negative.

4. For details, see W. Leonhard, *Kreml ohne Stalin* (Cologne, 1959), especially pp. 122–147, 211–225, 340–347, 382–406.

5. See, for example, Z. Mlynář; *Krize v sovětských systémech 1953–1981* (Köln: Index, 1983). Note, in particular, the chapter on the relative stabilization of the Soviet system in the 1970s.

6. Mikhail Gorbachev has repeatedly stated that there is no alternative to the perestroika policy except stagnation and the end of the USSR as a world power. See his speeches at the 27th Congress of CPSU (February 1986), at the plenary session of the CPSU Central Committee on the economy in June 1987, and again at the 19th All-Union Conference in June 1988. Also refer to his book *Perestroika* (London: Fontana/Collins, 1988).

7. The educational status of people employed in the USSR is summarized as follows:

Per thousand employees in	1959	1979
University students	33	100
Technical college students	76	167
High school students	64	276
Students who did not finish high school	260	262
Junior high (and lower) education	567	195

Quoted in *Sozialismus*, Nos. 7–8 (1986), p. 75.

8. "A society or community that is to govern itself must receive all the time a full flow of three kinds of information: firstly, information about the outside world; secondly, information about the past, with a wide spread of evocations and new combinations; thirdly, information about itself and its own past. Should any of these three streams be interrupted for long, for instance by suppression or concealment, the society would become an automaton or walking corpse. It would lose control over its own behavior not only in some of its parts, but over itself as

a whole." See K. W. Deutsch, *Nervy vlády* (Prague, 1971), pp. 215–216.

9. In this connection, Mikhail Gorbachev writes of a "braking mechanism" in his book *Perestroika*, p. 19.

10. The first such radical criticism of the "braking mechanism" to appear in the Soviet press was that by A. Butenko in the journal *Moskovskiye novosti* (25 October 1987). Since then it has become quite common and is repeatedly voiced.

11. In a 1985 interview in *l'Humanité*, Gorbachev referred to "Stalinism" as a product of Western journalists. And in a discussion with writers (which, though never published, was recorded in *samizdat* in 1986), he said that "the time for the past will come," but everything must "be taken in order" and the main thing now is the present and the future.

12. See the speech by Gorbachev at the January meeting of the CPSU Central Committee 1987, published in *Komunist* (in Russian), No. 2 (1987).

13. "Even the grossest mistakes, even the departure from the principles of socialism which have occurred could not deflect our people and our country from the path they entered upon by the choice made in 1917." See *Komunist*, No. 17 (1987), p. 15.

14. For more details, see Ch. Schmidt-Häuer and M. Huber, *Russland's zweite Revolution* (Munich 1987), p. 154 *et seq.*

15. See V. I. Lenin: *Left-Wing Communism: An Infantile Disorder* New York: International Publishers Co., 1940), written in 1920.

16. "Comrades, I want to emphasize once more that our attention to history is not motivated simply by an interest in the past. It is quite essential for our present work, for tackling the tasks of restructuring. We have declared the slogan: 'More socialism!'—and we have to recognize what values and principles should be regarded today as truly socialist." See *Komunist*, No. 4 (1988), p. 11. Compare this view of the matter with that described in Note 11.

17. The first to formulate this problem so radically was A. Yakovlev. His speech was published in the USSR only in the journal *Komunist Tadzhikistana* (April 1987).

18. See Gorbachev's speech at the CPSU Central Committee meeting of 18 February 1988, published in *Komunist*, No. 4 (1988).

19. In particular, see the resolutions of the 27th CPSU Congress (February 1986) and the measures decided by the plenary meeting of the CPSU Central Committee (CC) on economic reform in June 1987. In the political area, see the documents of the CC meeting in February 1988 and those of the 19th All-Union Congress in June 1988.

20. In my view, the new reform ideology will not be able to manage without defining in ideological terms the necessary relationships between the autonomy of those who are "managed" and the ability of the social entity to "manage itself." To cross Marx's and Lenin's ideas with scientific management theory (as has been done by the so-called political cybernetics [see Deutsch, *Nervy vlády*]) is very difficult but not impossible. For instance, Marx's fundamental ideas about centralism in the system of "self-management of the commune type" proceed from the necessary autonomy of those who are actually managed in "the cybernetic sense." However, Marx saw the problems of the social forms and aspects of "voluntary centralism" in what is from the standpoint of present-day society a utopian manner.

21. "The Party could not have risen so high in importance and could not have overshadowed all other forms of organization of the proletariat, if the latter had not been confronted with the problem of power, if the conditions of imperialism, the inevitability of wars, and the existence of a crisis had not demanded the concentration of all the forces of the proletariat at one point, the gathering of all the threats of the revolutionary movements in one spot in order to overthrow the bourgeoisie and to achieve the dictatorship of the proletariat." See J. Stalin, The Foundations of Leninism [1924], in *Problems of Leninism* (Moscow, 1958), p. 105.

22. In 1921 the Bolshevik party had more than 500,000 members. Of these, some 160,000 were expelled during the purges of "careerists." Pre-revolution Bolsheviks made up only 12 percent of the membership. See *Die Sowjetunion—Dokumente* (Munich, 1986), p. 53.

23. The strongest criticism of the process of subordinating the revolutionary masses to party officials was made by Rosa Luxemburg. See, for instance, L. Kolakowski, *Die Haupströmungen des Marxismus*, part 2 (Munich, 1982), p. 99 *et seq.*

24. As subsequent developments have shown, Gorbachev's idea involves a certain "subordination" of leading party officials to the Soviets and, hence, also control by the voters. This idea is inconsistent and not very clear; we shall deal with it in greater detail in the third section of this chapter, "The Law-Based State in the Soviet System."

25. See *Pravda* (1 October 1988).

26. Such a proposal was occasionally made in discussion prior to the 19th All-Union Conference of the CPSU. See *Komunist*, No. 3 (1988), p. 35 *et seq.*

27. The draft statutes of the Czechoslovak Communist party recognized the right of minority views to exist in the party, but it did not allow for activity by factions.

28. To express such a view in the USSR meant for many decades to risk being accused of Trotskyism, with all the attendant consequences. (In Stalin's days the risk was literally a danger to life.) After Gorbachev's accession, this view initially appeared (as far as I know) in the party press in an article by Tatyana Zaslavskaya. See *Komunist*, No. 13 (1986). Since then it has frequently also been voiced as a radical criticism of the Soviet bureaucracy.

29. *Komunist*, No. 13 (1986), p. 66.

30. Lenin did not, however, reject the basic necessity for feedback. For instance, during a discussion of trade unions in 1921, he emphasized that "trade unions are definitely obliged to defend the interests of the workers . . . [and] constantly to correct mistakes and excesses insofar as they are caused by bureaucratic distortions of the state apparatus." Yet in Stalin's writings we find nothing about the need for feedback.

31. In his speeches at the Komsomol Congress and the Trade Union Congress in 1987, Gorbachev spoke especially about the need of their officials for greater independent responsibility, in opposition to the endeavor by the party apparatus to limit the independence of these organizations.

32. The subject of so-called nonformal organizations is dealt with by O. G. Rumyantsev in *O samodeyatelnom dvizhenii ob-shestvennykh initsiativ—Institut Ekonomiki Mirovoy Sotsialisti-cheskoy Sistemy A.N.—USSR* (Moscow, 1988). This work was published by the USSR Academy of Sciences in the form of photocopies and is thus considered "semi-official."

33. From the end of the nineteenth century to the middle of the twentieth, the proportion of Russians in the USSR (previously the Russian empire) steadily increased. In the 1950s, a reverse trend started; by 1979, Russians constituted only 52.4 percent of the USSR population. See *Sowjetunion* (1986–1987), p. 89.

34. Under pressure from nationality conflicts, especially between Armenians and Azerbaidzhanis, and in the Baltic Republics in 1988, the CPSU Central Committee decided to hold a special meeting on the subject. There was to have been a critical analysis of the situation and proposals for a range of measures (from economic to legal) capable of reducing and, in time, eliminating the tension. But the meeting was postponed to late 1988.

35. For more details, see W. Brus: *Geschichte der Wirtschafts-politik in Osteuropa* (Cologne, 1986).

36. Gorbachev usually refers in this connection to Marx's statements about the alienation of producers from the means of production. But whereas Marx deals with the means of over-coming this alienation throughout the industrial reproduction process, Gorbachev often simplifies the problem (while still using Marxist phraseology) in terms of the individual producer's re-lationship to the instruments of production that he employs. For him, the leasing of land to peasant families thus overcomes the producer's alienation from the instruments of production. Al-though this is the case in a narrow sense, Gorbachev's argument would cause Marx to turn in his grave—particularly if it is declared to be a means of putting his theoretical ideas into practice.

37. "Self-management by work teams" has not yet become a subject of practical discussion in the USSR; it has been confined to the question of electing leading officials in enterprises. In the discussions on reforming the political system at the 19th Party Conference in June 1988, the subject was barely mentioned.

Ideas about the need to link producers' self-management with the institutions of political democracy, which were typical of the proposals put forward by the reform communists in Czechoslovakia in 1968, have not yet emerged in the USSR.

38. See the more detailed argument from the standpoint of a normative concept of law written by O. Weinberger, *Abstimmungslogik und Demokratie*, in *Reformen des Rechts* (Graz, 1979), p. 606.

39. See the resolutions of the 19th All-Union Conference of the CPSU in June 1988, published in *Komunist*, No. 10 (1988), p. 70.

40. See the Constitution of the RSFSR of 1918, published in *Die Sowjetunion*, Vol. 1: Documents (Munich: H. Altrichter, 1987), p. 132 *et seq.*

41. Lenin dealt with this subject in the well-known articles he wrote just before his death. (Particularly relevant is the article "How to Organize the Workers' and Peasants' Inspection.") See editions of Lenin's works.

42. The proposals for amending the Constitution and the electoral law, which have since been published, unfortunately contain no explicit guarantees against such manipulations by the political (party) apparatus. Only the opportunity to choose among several candidates is clearly guaranteed. The right to nominate candidates will still be confined to "work teams" and "voters' meetings" without any more precise legal definition included in the law. The possibility remains that the participants in these meetings may be manipulated. A new feature is the right for "social organizations" to nominate candidates. (In some cases a quota will be assigned to certain organizations.) Of course, the reference here is only to the enormous official "mass organizations," with their inner structures subject to "democratic centralism." See *Pravda* (22 and 23 October 1988).

43. See Gorbachev's speech at the 19th All-Union Conference of the CPSU, published in *Komunist*, No. 10 (1988), p. 31.

44. This principle was explicitly embodied in, for instance, the Action Program of the Communist party of Czechoslovakia of 5 April 1968.

45. See the resolutions of the 19th All-Union Conference of the CPSU, published in *Komunist*, No. 10 (1988), pp. 69–70.

46. Ibid., p. 87.

47. See the discussion on legal reform in *Pravda* (2 August 1988).

48. For further details regarding the development of the theoretical concept of law in the USSR and the role of A. J. Vishynsky's concepts, see Dieter Pfaff: *Die Entwicklung der sowjetischen Rechhtslehre* (Cologne, 1968).

49. See the resolutions of the 19th All-Union Conference of the CPSU, published in an article entitled "On Legal Reform," *Komunist*, No. 10 (1988), p. 85.

50. See the report of Shevardnadze's speech in *Pravda* (26 July 1988), p. 4. For a fuller version of the speech, see *Vestnik Ministerstva inostrannykh del SSSR* (August 1988), pp. 27–46.

51. I think that Gorbachev himself demonstrates this point in *Perestroika*, pp. 135–244.

52. See, for example, D. Senghaas, *Die Zukunft Europas* (Frankfurt, 1986), p. 33. For an overall review, see Czempiel et al., "Amerikanische Aussenpolitik in den siebziger Jahren," in *Politik und Wirtschaft in den USA* (Bonn: Bundeszentrale f. politische Bildung, 1984), p. 97 *et seq.*

53. See M. Görtemaker, *Die Unheilige Allianz* (Munich, 1979), p. 101 *et seq.*

54. See the draft materials for the 19th All-Union Conference of the CPSU, as well as Gorbachev's report to this conference, in *Komunist*, No. 10 (1988).

55. For further details, see K. W. Deutsch, *Analyse internationaler Beziehungen* (Frankfurt, 1968).

56. Of course, there was no mention at all of the fact that identical or similar ideas were openly persecuted as being "non-class thinking" and thus heresy against Marxism-Leninism.

57. See the new (February 1986) version of the CPSU program, published in *Komunist*, No. 4 (1986).

58. Editor V. Afanasyev, *Pravda* (5 December 1986).

59. See Gorbachev's political report to the CPSU 27th Congress, published in *Komunist*, No. 4 (1986).

60. See the speeches by Gorbachev and Ligachev to the CPSU 27th Congress, published in *Pravda* (7 November 1986).

61. See the 1961 version of the CPSU program.

62. See the 1986 version of the CPSU program.

63. Shevardnadze, *Pravda* (26 July 1988).

64. See the report of a speech by J. Ligachev in the town of Gorky, published in *Pravda* (6 August 1988).

65. Lenin "spoke more than once about the priority of interests common to all humanity over class interests," as Gorbachev writes in his book *Perestroika*, p. 145. He repeated this statement many times in various speeches, and it is quoted by many authors.

66. See the article by Editor Afanasyev in *Pravda* (5 December 1986).

67. See the statement by Shevardnadze in *Pravda* (27 July 1988).

68. On this, see, for example, Francis Fukuyama, *Gorbatchow und die dritte Welt, Europäische Rundschau*, No. 3, quoted in *Foreign Affairs* (New York, Spring 1986).

69. See the statement by Shevardnadze in *Pravda* (26 July 1988).

70. See Gorbachev's speech on the occasion of the 70th anniversary of the October Socialist Revolution, published in *Komunist*, No. 17 (1986), pp. 32–34.

71. *Pravda* (26 July 1988).

72. Henry Kissinger and Cyrus Vance, "Amerika's Auftrag nach Ronald Reagan," *Die Zeit* (17 June 1988). An abbreviated version is published as "Bipartisan Objectives for American Foreign Policy," *Foreign Affairs* 66, no. 5 (Summer 1988), pp. 899–921.

73. *Beijing Rundschau*, No. 33 (16 August 1988), p. 31.

74. See the 1986 version of the CPSU program.

75. See the detailed analysis of development in Soviet-bloc countries after 1945 in Hartmann's *Politik und Gesellschaft in Osteuropa*.

76. See, for instance, Senghaas, in *Die Zukunft Europas*, on the "Finlandization" of Eastern Europe.

77. See, for example, E. Eppler, "Friedenspolitik und Ideologie," *Mediatus,* No. 4 (1986).

78. For a contemporary review of the problems, see, for instance, the collection published by Rolf Schlüter, *Wirtschaftsreformen im Ostblock in den 80er Jahren* (Schöning-Verlag, Paderborn-Wien-Zürich, 1988).

79. Resolution of this situation without upheaval will require a compromise between the government and Solidarity. The latter was forcibly repressed seven years ago but has not ceased to exist. What would appear to be possible in this connection is difficult (even unattainable) due to the elements of political prestige that have been present in the Polish conflict from 1980 to this day.

80. For a detailed account of this subject, see Zdeněk Mlynář; *Bilance politiky "Pražského jara" po dvaceti letech* (address to the seminar at the Gramsci Institute, Bologna, on 8 July 1988), published in *Listy* No. 5 (1988).

81. See, for example, V. Semenichin's statement in *Pravda* (10 April 1989), p. 3.

82. See the resolution of the CPSU Central Committee of 16 March 1989, published in *Pravda* (1 April 1989).

83. See the speech by Shevardnadze at the session of the Central Committee of the Georgian Communist party on 14 April 1989, published in *Pravda* (16 April 1989).

84. See *Budapester Rundschau* (20 February 1989), p. 3.

85. See *Pravda* (8 December 1988).

86. See Gorbachev's speech given at a luncheon with Margaret Thatcher, published in *Pravda* (7 April 1989).

Index